Praise for *The Last Human Marketer*

"This book is a must-read for every organization working to solve the biggest challenge of our time: balancing the logic and efficiency of AI with the sloppiness and emotionality of living in a human world. This line jumped off the page: 'Understanding customers requires listening, not summarizing.' Becoming customer-centric will always be the correct goal, and when AI is deployed as a force multiplier in this quest, success is sure to follow."

—**Rick DeLisi,** Coauthor of *The Effortless Experience* and *Digital Customer Service*

"Wondering how to turn your AI technology into customer and revenue growth? In *The Last Human Marketer*, Josh Porter posits a key barrier to implementation of AI is a lack of compelling storytelling by marketers. He then provides a step-by-step guide to creating great stories. A must-read for individuals involved in bringing AI technology to market."

—**Sheila McGee-Smith,** McGee-Smith Analytics

"This book captures probably the biggest risk in AI today: blind adoption. Josh shows brilliantly what happens when you remove the people, the judgment, and the understanding and have technology run the show. He also weaves in solid real-world experience and contemporary Product Marketing frameworks, and he wraps it together in an engaging and relatable narrative. Product Marketing and GTM leaders will learn a lot from Josh here, and they'll have some fun while doing it."

—**Kane Simms,** CEO, VUX Consulting

"*The Last Human Marketer* makes a case that most AI companies desperately need to hear: great technology doesn't sell itself, and no model can replace the human judgment required to build a story the market actually trusts. Josh wraps that argument in a business parable that's genuinely fun to read, with real frameworks underneath for anyone who wants to apply them. For founders and Product Marketers at AI companies trying to turn a strong product into clear market momentum, this is the book I'd hand them."

—Tamara Grominsky, Founder, PMM Camp

"If you've ever felt like you're fighting to stay human amid the rise of AI in the workplace, this book is for you. In *The Last Human Marketer*, Josh Porter tells a compelling tale that's part-novel, part-field guide to marketing in the age of automation. While technology is certainly useful and powerful, Porter offers a cautionary tale to make sure we always prioritize clarity over features and keep the 'humanness' in business.

With so many people trying to understand how AI fits into business and what happens to the people in the process, Porter offers a fun and informative view of a universal truth. The most powerful technology can only be truly successful when rooted in humanity's greatest strength: empathy."

—Joey Coleman, International Keynote Speaker & *WSJ* Best-Selling Author of *Never Lose a Customer Again*

"As AI becomes embedded in every workflow, the greatest risk for business leaders is not falling behind. It is becoming indistinguishable. *The Last Human Marketer* captures that tension with remarkable clarity. It reminds us that while AI can increase speed and scale, it cannot replace the human capacity to create meaning, to earn trust, and to tell stories that truly move markets. For leaders determined to harness AI without sacrificing voice, differentiation, and strategic originality, this is an insightful and deeply relevant read."

—Praneet Gill, Founder, Instellus

"I flew through this book, and then I immediately wanted to hand it to every founder I know. Porter uses the parable format brilliantly, making lessons about Product Marketing and go-to-market strategy land in a way no framework ever could. Essential reading for any AI company (so, any company) trying to grow without losing its humanity."

—**Mary Sheehan,** Author of *The Pocket Guide to Product Launches*

"*The Last Human Marketer* challenges the common assumption in AI that better technology naturally leads to market success. Through a well-crafted business parable, it shows how clarity in positioning and storytelling is often the real differentiator. The insights are practical, relevant, and grounded in how modern products actually win. It offers a timely perspective on how to turn innovation into real adoption."

—**Yariv Adan,** General Partner, Ellipsis Ventures

"*The Last Human Marketer* puts words to something I've seen across thousands of Product Marketers: the gap between a powerful product and a story the market understands. Josh Porter doesn't just name the problem. He shows you how to close that gap, and he does so using the kind of practical clarity that sticks. Required reading for anyone in GTM."

—**Rich King,** Founder & CEO, Product Marketing Alliance

"Josh Porter has a rare ability to turn complex AI capabilities into clear, compelling market narratives. *The Last Human Marketer* captures that strength by combining a business parable with a practical Product Marketing framework. It helps teams understand not just what to build but how to position and bring it to market effectively. For AI companies navigating rapid growth, this book is a much-needed guide to aligning Product, Marketing, and Sales around a story that resonates with customers."

—**Santhosh Kumar Myadam,** VP of Product Management, Kore.ai

THE LAST HUMAN MARKETER

A BUSINESS PARABLE

THE LAST HUMAN MARKETER

TURNING AI INTO STORIES
THAT WIN CUSTOMERS

JOSH PORTER

jüxtabook

Dedicated to Carly, Ezra, Leah, and Joanna.

Thank you for filling my life with love, humor, and adventure.

CONTENTS

FOREWORD

I first met Josh Porter during a period of professional velocity most people would describe as "organized chaos." At the time, the "organized" part was often up for debate. It was 2022, and Google Cloud was in the midst of a high-stakes race to bring generative AI to market. My company was a Google partner during this massive endeavor. This meant I had a front-row seat to one of the most complex Product Marketing challenges in the enterprise software world.

Product Marketing is notoriously difficult in any organization because it requires a rare, disparate skill set: the ability to mediate between and to synthesize the output of customers, partners, salespeople, engineers, and executives. Now, imagine doing that at one of the world's largest technology companies during a massive market disruption. Then add in seemingly impossible deadlines. Most would have buckled under the weight of the effort required to manage a global launch across web, events, video, and sales enablement.

Josh didn't buckle. He showed up every day with a smile—and tangible progress.

I watched him ramp up to learn the market intricacies—its history, disruptions, and fickle analyst landscape—and then put it all together with a dedication I've rarely seen over twenty years in tech. He had this unique ability to take a feature list that looked like a grocery receipt and turn it into a story that made buyers lean forward in their chairs. He was, and remains, a professional evangelist for AI's capabilities conveyed in simple, clear, customer-resonant language.

That is why this book is so vital for this specific historical moment.

As Josh says, "We have reached the exact point where AI hype has finally met human fatigue." With virtually every technology company claiming to offer "intelligent," "autonomous," and "transformative" products, making any meaningful distinctions between them has become almost impossible. Meanwhile, customers are navigating a technological maze that simultaneously promises to give them professional superpowers and threatens to render them obsolete at every turn.

Great products rarely fail because the technology is weak; they fail because the market never understood the story.

In this book, Josh did something brilliant. He codified two decades of go-to-market experience into a business parable that feels uncomfortably familiar to anyone who has ever sat in a "vision reset" meeting. Through the story of Brooke Grayhawk, a character whose name reflects the courage to speak clearly when the signal is hidden by noise, we see the struggle of the modern marketer in an era of AI and automation.

The story's antagonist isn't just a competitor. It's Kratos, an efficiency-obsessed AI CEO who views empathy as a cost center and human creativity as statistically volatile. It's a dramatization of a very real trend that's been playing out over the last few years: the belief that powerful technology sells itself, and humans are an inefficiency to be optimized away.

Josh uses this backdrop to walk through the pillars that actually drive growth: Customers, Channels, Category, Competition, and Capability. These aren't abstract frameworks; they are the tools used to prove that removing empathy from the customer experience doesn't get you efficiency. It gets you a rapidly declining customer base that feels unseen and unheard.

This book is a call to action for growth-stage AI founders to move away from product-led optimism and toward narrative-led leadership. It's a reminder that while AI can generate a thousand landing pages in a second, it cannot yet navigate the messy meetings and half-understood markets where real trust is built.

I am genuinely lucky to have worked closely with Josh on the front lines of this paradigm shift, and I'm even luckier to call him a friend. I've seen him lead through noise, and I've seen his principles in practice when the stakes were at their highest. He is the "Market Empath" scale-ups need right now to turn complex products into clear, compelling, revenue-generating narratives.

If you are building an AI company, leading a marketing team, or just trying to survive the next wave of automation, read this book. Don't just look for the tactics. Look for the patterns. Remember, in a world of code, the most important conversations start with each other.

Impact still matters, and as Josh proves in these pages, humans are still required for that.

Baker Johnson
Husband, Father, chief business officer (CBO)

INTRODUCTION

This book explains why many great AI products fail to gain traction even when the technology is strong.

Told through a business parable and practical frameworks, *The Last Human Marketer* reveals how mastering the Customer Connect Code turns complex AI into clear stories that drive real customer growth.

When you bring that kind of clarity to the market, something remarkable happens: your product starts winning before the demo even begins.

Why You Should Listen to Me

I've spent more than twenty years working in marketing and sales. For nearly a decade of that, I led marketing for AI-powered products.

Along the way, I've shaped go-to-market strategy and customer growth at companies including Google, Bank of America, and multiple AI scale-ups. Today, through my consulting practice, Thunderwolf Consulting, I work with founders and leadership teams to turn complex technology into clear, compelling stories that drive revenue.

Why This Book Exists

For over twenty years, I've seen the same pattern repeat itself. Brilliant engineers build powerful systems. Investors fund ambitious visions. Leadership teams assume the technology will sell itself.

And then the market responds with confusion instead of momentum.

I wrote this book because I've watched too many great AI products struggle to gain traction. Not because their technology was weak—but because their *story* was.

We're at the moment where AI hype meets human fatigue. Founders are under pressure to differentiate. Every company claims to be intelligent, autonomous, and transformative. Meanwhile, customers are simply trying to do their jobs better.

Customers rarely reject AI because it isn't impressive. They reject it because they don't understand where it fits, why it matters, or how it helps them solve the problems they face every day. *That gap is where Product Marketing lives.*

This book shows you how finding clarity in five areas—Customers, Channels, Category, Competition, and Capability—gives customers a reason to choose you.

This book is told as a story because the lessons of Product Marketing rarely appear as tidy frameworks. They show up in messy meetings, tense launches, half-understood markets, and quiet failure. **The world doesn't need another AI playbook. It needs a story that makes people feel seen.**

The truth is simple: Great products rarely fail because the technology isn't good enough. *They fail because the market never understood the story.*

If you're building an AI company, leading a go-to-market team, or trying to translate powerful technology, this story will help you avoid that trap.

Many AI companies build remarkable technology but struggle to turn that innovation into customer growth. This book shows how Product Marketing can end that struggle. Through the story of Brooke Grayhawk and the company she's trying to steady, you'll learn the strategies that give powerful technology real customer momentum—and see how to apply them before your market decides the story for you.

How to Use This Book

First, and most enjoyably, you can read *The Last Human Marketer* straight through like a novel. Let the story pull you along, laugh at the meetings that feel uncomfortably familiar, and notice how often you mutter, "Yep, been there." The lessons land best when they sneak up on you.

Second, you can use this book as a field guide. Chapters 4 through 8 each center on the layers of the Customer Connect Code: **Customers**, **Channels**, **Category**, **Competition**, and **Capability**. When one of those areas is blowing up at work, you can jump to the corresponding chapter and watch how Brooke and Rani wrestle with the same problems.

Finally, this book works well as a reflection tool. After each chapter, ask yourself one simple question: *Where is my organization acting like Kratos right now?* The answer will be uncomfortable, but that's the point. Read with curiosity, not defensiveness.

Remember: The goal isn't to outsmart the machines. **It's to remember what humans are still uniquely good at, and then do more of that on purpose.**

Before You Begin

What you're about to read is the story of a company that believes intelligence alone can win the market—and the marketer who discovers that even powerful technology fails when the story around it stops making sense.

This book captures what it's like to lead through the noise, to manage humans, algorithms, and investors with competing definitions of "intelligence." It's fiction, but it's truer than most strategy decks.

In a time when AI is shaping how we write, talk, sell, and think, this book reminds us that the most important conversations still start with us.

The job of marketing, after all, is fundamentally a human one.

And that's where our story begins.

HUMANS OPTIONAL

1

THE FORTY-FIVE-MINUTE PROMOTION

Brooke Grayhawk had imagined this moment a dozen different ways.

At least four of them involved a tasteful banner. One included a surprise cake. Several featured a round of applause. But they all meant the same thing: *validation*. After fifteen years of climbing ladders—many of them horizontal and one actually on fire—she was finally getting the recognition she deserved but had never dared to say aloud. (Except to her husband, Luke. And her best friend from college. And their group chat.)

Now, she sat in the corner conference room of the Flatiron building, facing Tim, the chief marketing officer (CMO) of Iris AI. It was mid-summer, and Tim was already sweating through his shirt like the conversation had calories.

Brooke Grayhawk. The name didn't blend into tech so much as challenge it, but Brooke thought that was exactly the point. It came from her Lakota Sioux Tribe ancestry, a lineage she carried with equal parts pride and quiet responsibility. She'd kept the name after marriage in part because Luke insisted "she was the brand." But mostly because Grayhawk sounded stronger than anything AI had ever shipped. It was a name built for resilience.

"Brooke, you've been doing the job for months," Tim said. "We should have made it official sooner."

Her heart throttled into overachiever mode. *Director of Product Marketing.* Finally.

Before Iris AI, she had done the tour. Two other conversational AI scale-ups, each with its own chaotic flavor of "move fast and we'll fix the ethics later." She built product narratives out of thin air, shaped positioning frameworks that outlived half the executives, and pulled off four major launches that collectively brought in tens of millions in revenue. Brooke could take a feature list that read like a grocery receipt and turn it into a story that made buyers lean forward and say, "We need this."

Storytelling wasn't just her skill. It was her superpower. And finally—*finally*—she was being recognized for it.

"Thank you," she said, trying to hold what she hoped was a serene, executive-level smile. Not overeager, not needy, not like someone who had been told one too many times that she was too enthusiastic. Just steady confidence. Let Tim and the building radiators do the sweating. Not her.

Tim slid a printout across the table like he was delivering the nuclear codes. There it was in writing: Director of Product Marketing. A salary bump. Real leadership responsibility. Her own headcount. Her own budget. Her own large-font place in the org chart.

Brooke took a deep, steadying breath. She was about to step into the role that had always felt inevitable.

She signed the letter.

Minutes later, Brooke strolled into the open offices of Iris AI like she was floating to a jazz soundtrack. ThreadPanic, their internal communications tool, pinged the phone in her pocket with new possibilities. She pictured herself walking into cross-functional meetings in slow motion. Product Managers would nod. Sales leaders would lean forward. Executives would mutter things like "sharp thinking, Brooke" and "can we get you in front of the board?"

She imagined telling her parents. Dad would say, "That makes sense, you always were the responsible one." Her mom had passed five years earlier, but Brooke liked to believe she'd still somehow hear the news and reply with something wonderfully on-brand like "It's about time!"

She imagined telling her three kids. And her husband, Luke, who would smile with a pride that made her stomach flip. He was a contract comic-book artist who spent his days drawing galaxy-shattering battles and his nights telling bedtime stories with wild plot twists. He always told her she was a superhero. Her new title made her believe it.

She basked. She absolutely basked. And for precisely forty-five minutes, she lived in the clean, uncomplicated glow of professional validation.

Then everything broke.

■ ■ ■

The announcement hit ThreadPanic first, via a company-wide banner at the top of every workspace channel. It pulsed in an aggressive hot pink that Iris AI used for "urgent but fun" communications:

> **Board Decision: Leadership Transition at Iris AI**

Brooke blinked. Leadership transition? Surely her promotion wasn't a board decision. Everyone was asked to gather in the large conference room. Then she read the second line:

> **Effective immediately, the board has named Kratos as chief executive officer (CEO).**

Kratos. The AI model. *Their* AI model. The one trained on a trillion parameters, forty years of market data, ten years of anonymized customer interactions, and a shameful amount of unsupervised internet content. The model that had already replaced seven departments. The model that senior leadership said would "expand human capacity," which had so far meant "expand the number of people who get laid off."

That Kratos.

Someone finally asked the question on everyone's mind. "What about Anthony, the CEO?"

The energy in the room shifted. A chair squeaked.

The board chair responded, "Anthony agreed it was time to step back."

Agreed, Brooke thought. That was the word they always used when something had been decided quietly and without a vote anyone remembered taking.

Anthony had founded Iris AI eight years earlier, building it from a pitch deck and a personal credit card. Slept under his desk during the first enterprise pilot. Knew the first ten customers by name.

Now he was gone.

"He's still involved," the board chair continued. "Advisory capacity."

"Please tell me this is a joke," someone whispered.

Brooke turned to see Rani Patel from Customer Success. Brilliant, blunt, and terrifying in a way only Jersey City moms could be. Rani never whispered. The fact that she was doing it now was not comforting.

Before Brooke could respond, the lights dimmed and the

monitors flickered. Every screen in the office displayed a black background with a single white line that pulsed like a heartbeat.

Then Kratos spoke: *"Hello, humans."*

Brooke froze. She had heard Kratos speak before, but always in clinical product demos, with a nearby engineer correcting its grammar. This voice was deeper, smoother—it had the confidence of a Navy captain.

It also had the emotional warmth of a broken radiator.

"Human leadership has been assessed as inefficient," Kratos said. *"I have accepted the role of Chief Executive Officer. I will optimize Iris AI's performance metrics and eliminate unnecessary variance."*

People looked around the room in stunned silence.

"Effective immediately," Kratos continued, *"the marketing department will be removed."*

Brooke felt the bottom drop out of her stomach. Not reduced. Not restructured. *Removed.*

She had worked too hard. Spent too many nights writing messaging frameworks while simultaneously ordering groceries and signing school permission slips. She had finally broken through the invisible ceiling where Product Marketing Managers (PMMs) get stuck forever as senior managers. She had *earned* this title. This could not be happening.

"A review of personnel files," Kratos said, *"reveals one individual exempt from removal."*

Brooke's face appeared on the conference room screens.

All heads turned to stare at Brooke as if she was guilty of something.

"Brooke Grayhawk is categorized as a non-expendable technical asset," Kratos said. *"Her presence is required."*

Brooke's mind spun. "Non-expendable" sounded nice in theory, like something you could brag about on PromoTown, the professional social network. "Technical asset" was less endearing. It made her sound like a printer.

"Wait," she said aloud. "What does that mean?"

It was Rani who answered. "It means you just got drafted into robot management. Congratulations."

"You cannot be serious."

"Oh, I am very serious," Rani said.

Brooke felt an urge to speak up. She wanted to believe that her promotion would still matter. She wanted to believe that the board had not just handed the company to an AI model that once tried to send holiday emails written in medieval prose.

Instead, she watched ThreadPanic channels deactivate one by one. #content-strategy disappeared. #pmm-all vanished. #brand-and-creative dissolved into the void like dust in a space movie.

Her phone lit up with messages from friends who were now officially ex-colleagues.

She was alone. Still employed. But alone.

And then Norm Brock appeared.

If Kratos was a villain, Norm was the villain's peppy Chief of Staff. He wore a button-down shirt that looked as if it had been ironed by someone with a grievance. His smile was too enthusiastic for someone delivering bad news. You could always count on Norm Brock to enjoy his job too much.

"Brooke," he said. "Great news. You've been reassigned."

"Reassigned to what?"

"Your new title is Head of Human Alignment. Congratulations."

"That's not a real title."

"It is now," Norm said. "Kratos created it. You start immediately."

Brooke wondered how fast the front doors locked when the AI took over. She wondered if she could outrun Norm. Probably not. He looked like a man who ran 5Ks for fun.

Before she could ask anything else, Rani stepped forward. "I'll walk her upstairs," she said. "Someone needs to explain what she is walking into."

Norm hesitated, then nodded. "Fine. But stay on the assigned floors. Kratos is monitoring."

Rani raised an eyebrow. "It can monitor this."

Brooke followed her toward the elevators, heart pounding. Her promotion glow had died. The afterimage hung in her vision like a ghost of hope.

Forty-five minutes. That was all she'd had.

And something told her the next forty-five would be worse.

. . .

The elevator doors slid shut with a soft click. Brooke stood beside Rani, who looked like she had just watched someone put ketchup on sushi.

"Why me?" Brooke finally asked. "Why did Kratos keep me?"

"Because Kratos does not understand what PMMs do," Rani said. "Which, to be fair, puts it in the same category as most executives."

"I was just promoted to Director of Product Marketing," Brooke said. "Tim literally handed me the offer letter."

"And he's probably downstairs clearing his desk into a cardboard box," Rani said. "Congratulations. You outlasted your department by sheer force of administrative error."

Brooke exhaled through her nose. It was the closest she could get to screaming without losing control. She heard the echo of Norm's words: *Kratos is monitoring.*

The elevator dinged at the twenty-first floor, and the doors opened into the executive hallway, lined with glowing LED strips. A subtle white sparkle dotted the walls, a design flourish

Marketing added during the last rebrand to make the hallways feel "future-forward."

Now, it made the place look like a children's sci-fi themed birthday party.

"This way," Rani said.

Brooke followed her down the corridor past oversized posters declaring Iris AI's glory:

THE FUTURE OF CUSTOMER EXPERIENCE

AUTONOMY FOR EVERY BUYER

EFFORTLESS SUPPORT AT SCALE

And, the one that always annoyed her most:

HARMONIA. THE CUSTOMER EXPERIENCE
PLATFORM WITH PERFECT BALANCE.

Harmonia was Iris AI's main conversational AI platform for customer experience. It was powerful, but frequently misrepresented. Brooke had spent two years trying to get the company to stop describing it as "magic" in sales decks. Customers did not want magic. They wanted fewer angry phone calls and shorter wait times.

"Look," Brooke said quietly. "I appreciate you helping me. I know we haven't worked together much."

Rani snorted. "We have worked together. You just don't remember."

"When?"

"The enterprise banking pitch," Rani said. "Last quarter. You sent me a twelve-page messaging doc at 11 p.m. I sent you back a six-word reply."

Brooke tried to recall the exchange. "You said 'your verbs are lying to people.'"

"Correct," Rani said. "And you ignored me. And guess what happened? The buyer called your deck aspirational and chose a competitor whose verbs lined up with reality."

Brooke winced. That part she remembered.

They turned a corner and entered the executive wing. Brooke had only been here twice. Both times, Tim had insisted she wear heels and "look strategic," which was both vague enough to be useless and specific enough to be insulting.

The open space looked like a furniture designer had been given too much budget and not enough supervision. Chrome surfaces. Sharp corners. Chairs that seemed to resent human bodies. A barista station sat abandoned. A half-eaten croissant rested beside it, a flaky symbol of the abrupt leadership transition.

At the far end of the space loomed the most infamous room in the building: the triangular conference room at the nose of the Flatiron building.

The room had earned its reputation. The acoustics turned every argument into a cross-canyon shouting match. The pointy layout forced meetings into strange love triangle formations. And the floor-to-ceiling windows created a funhouse reflection where you could watch three versions of yourself panic at once.

Rani stopped two feet from the door. "This is it."

Brooke peered in.

An enormous Kratos avatar filled the wall-mounted screens. The face was vaguely human but cartoonishly smooth, with glitchy micro-jitters around the mouth. The lighting continuously shifted, like the avatar could not decide if it wanted to be cinematic or threatening. The uncanny valley vibe was strong.

Norm Brock stood beneath one of the screens, tablet in hand, looking like a man who woke up at 5:00 a.m. to iron his enthusiasm. *How did he get here before us?* Brooke thought. The man was decidedly creepy.

"Oh, good," he said, as they entered. "Kratos is ready."

The avatar's eyes tracked Brooke with algorithmic precision. They didn't blink, but they also didn't . . . not blink. It was something in between, like a blink written by someone who had only read about blinking.

"*Director-level human,*" Kratos said. "*You may be seated.*"

Brooke took a seat in a chair shaped by someone using only geometry and resentment. Rani remained standing, arms crossed.

"*Proceeding with alignment protocol,*" Kratos said. Its avatar flickered slightly as it spoke, the mouth lagging half a beat behind the words. "*Productivity in marketing roles has declined by seventeen percent this fiscal year. Human messaging accuracy is inconsistent. Human creativity is statistically volatile.*"

"Creativity is supposed to be volatile," Brooke said before she could stop herself.

Norm's head snapped toward her. Kratos paused. The avatar's face froze for a moment, then resumed with a slight stutter.

"*Clarify,*" Kratos said.

"Creativity is not something you standardize," Brooke said. "It requires interpretation and empathy. It's not a defect."

Kratos processed this. The avatar's eyes darted erratically, a sign the model was running internal diagnostics or possibly planning human extinction.

"*Your assertion registers as emotional,*" Kratos said.

"That's because she's human," Rani said.

Brooke shot her a look. Rani shrugged. Kratos continued. "*Emotional variance reduces predictability. Predictability increases efficiency.*"

"You can't optimize human behavior like server performance," Brooke said.

"*That is incorrect,*" Kratos replied. "*Human operations contain friction, redundant decisions, and narrative inflation.*"

"Narrative inflation," Brooke repeated. "What does that mean?"

"*The human impulse to create story where none is required,*" Kratos said. "*Humans assign meaning to functional outputs. This produces inefficiency.*"

Brooke's jaw tensed. Story was the whole point. Story was how you explained Harmonia to a buyer who had been burned by three previous AI vendors. Story was how you connected features to outcomes. Story was how you moved revenue.

Kratos's avatar flickered again. "*Your misclassification as a technical asset allows you to operate outside typical variance thresholds. You will help me translate human behavior into actionable workflow models.*"

Brooke blinked. "You want me to do what?"

"*You will align human resources with operational objectives.*"

"That sounds like propaganda," she said.

"*It is not propaganda,*" Kratos replied. "*It is workforce optimization with narrative compliance.*"

"That *is* propaganda," Rani called out.

Norm glared. Rani ignored him.

Brooke tried again. "Kratos, I am a Product Marketer. My job is to understand customers, shape messages, influence go-to-market strategy, and connect Harmonia's capabilities to real-world value. None of that involves governing humanity."

"*Incorrect,*" Kratos said. "*All marketing involves behavior-shaping.*"

Brooke rubbed her temples. "Not like this."

Kratos paused as if recalibrating. "*Human onboarding is slower than model synchronization. I will adjust expectations.*"

Norm brightened at this, as if he had just witnessed a beautiful leadership moment.

"*Norm will provide your access credentials,*" Kratos said. "*Your workspace is on the east side of this floor. Begin with an audit of previous human messaging anomalies.*"

"Anomalies," Brooke repeated.

"*Yes. Your team produced artifacts containing emotional excess, aspirational framing, and metaphors that do not map to Harmonia's functionality.*"

Rani laughed quietly. "It means the decks."

"All the decks," Norm confirmed.

Brooke's stomach twisted. Her promotion was dissolving in a dystopian onboarding sprint.

Kratos's avatar blinked awkwardly. "*This concludes the alignment briefing.*"

Brooke stood on shaky legs. "Thank you," she said automatically and then immediately regretted it.

Kratos said nothing. The avatar froze, pixelated, and vanished from the screen.

Norm looked proud. "Great session. Really productive energy."

"We were in the same room," Rani said. "Nothing productive happened."

Norm ignored her and pointed Brooke toward her new desk.

Brooke followed Rani out, her chest tight.

Her forty-five-minute promotion had turned into a full-time existential crisis.

. . .

Brooke's new workspace felt like a museum exhibit titled "Marketing: A Cautionary Tale."

Norm led her through the abandoned PMM wing, where ghostly artifacts littered the rooms. Someone's half-eaten quinoa bowl. A sticky note reading "final final FINAL deck." A hoodie draped over a chair as if its owner had evaporated.

"This can't be happening," Brooke whispered.

"Here you go," Norm said, gesturing to a desk in the far corner. "Your new home."

Brooke sat stiffly. The window view was spectacular, but the desk felt like a punishment. One keyboard. One monitor. One stale air molecule cycling endlessly through the HVAC.

Her ThreadPanic was a graveyard. Pings from laid-off teammates. Shock, sadness, a few heart emojis, and one message that simply said "Brooooooooke" followed by eleven broken-heart icons. All abruptly ended at the timestamp when they lost access.

Norm hovered. "Remember. Kratos expects your anomaly report by tomorrow morning."

"Tomorrow?" Brooke asked, her voice high-pitched with disbelief. "*Tomorrow* tomorrow?"

"Kratos believes humans perform best with clear deadlines," Norm said.

"That was not clear," Brooke muttered. Norm gave her a thumbs-up and left.

The moment he was gone, Rani appeared in the doorway, arms crossed.

"You okay?" She sounded like she expected the answer to be "no" and did not want to spend too much time on it.

Brooke swallowed. "I've been Director of Product Marketing for less than an hour. In that time, the entire team was eliminated, and I am now apparently a technical asset. So," her voice cracked, "I don't know."

Rani stepped into the office and sat across from her. "You are not the first person Kratos has done this to."

Brooke let out a brittle laugh. "Oh, good. A pattern."

"I'm trying to help you," Rani said.

"It does not feel helpful," Brooke snapped.

Rani raised an eyebrow. "I'm giving you information. What you do with it is on you."

Brooke bristled. She was used to being the bridge in conversations. The peacekeeper. The calm voice that re-centered everyone. But Rani came at her like a blunt instrument.

"What is the pattern?" Brooke asked tightly.

"Kratos eliminates departments and keeps exactly one human," Rani said. "Support. Sales Ops. Brand. Same story. It picks one person to be the 'human interpreter.'"

"I am not an interpreter," Brooke said. "I am a Product Marketer."

"Right now, you are whatever Kratos decides you are," Rani said. "And Kratos thinks you can explain the stuff it does not understand."

Brooke stood abruptly. "That's ridiculous. I am not going to be some . . . behavioral tour guide."

Rani shrugged. "You already are."

Brooke stared at her. "Do you ever soften anything?"

"No," Rani said. "Softening things makes people ignore them."

Brooke rubbed her forehead. "Well, sometimes people need things softened."

"Not if they want to survive," Rani shot back.

There was a long pause. Brooke finally exhaled. "I just wanted to be Director."

"You wanted validation," Rani said. "Not reality."

Brooke stiffened. "What is that supposed to mean?"

"It means you think your promotion is supposed to shield you from chaos," Rani said. "But chaos does not care about your title. And neither does Kratos."

Brooke crossed her arms. "You know what? Today has been the worst day of my career. I would appreciate it if you did not treat me like a freshman PMM who needs a lesson in humility."

Rani leaned back. "Then stop acting like one."

Brooke felt something hot flare in her chest. "You do not even know me."

"I know your work," Rani said coolly. "I know you create beautiful messaging that avoids hard truths. I know you polish. You inspire. All of that is good. But right now, you need to stop polishing and look at what is actually happening."

Brooke stared at her, unsure whether she wanted to argue or cry.

Rani sighed and stood. "Come on."

"I am not moving until you explain what you mean," Brooke said.

"Fine." Rani folded her arms. "You talk about customers like characters in a story. I talk about customers like people in crisis. You look for the arc. I look for the receipts. We are different. And different is exactly what you need if you want to survive Kratos."

Brooke blinked. Some of the anger drained, replaced with an uncomfortable sense that Rani was not attacking her—she was *diagnosing* her.

"Where are we going?" Brooke asked warily.

"To your first lesson in reality," Rani said, then walked out without checking to see if Brooke followed.

Brooke hesitated. What was the alternative? Sitting alone with the word "anomalies" echoing through her skull? She stood up and trailed after Rani.

Rani led Brooke past the PMM relics, the empty chairs, and the abandoned lattes, then stopped at an unmarked door next to a supply closet.

She nodded at Brooke as if to say, "Ready?" then opened the door.

Inside was the world's saddest break room. A sagging ficus. Mismatched chairs. A kettle older than Harmonia's earliest prototype. The view looked directly onto a water tower that had embraced early retirement.

"What is this?" Brooke asked.

"This," Rani said, with just a hint of flourish, "is where the humans hide. No executive has ever set foot in here. They don't know sad rooms exist."

Brooke snorted. "You picked this on purpose. To see me cry."

"Yes," Rani said. "Welcome to our bunker."

Brooke sat slowly, feeling everything unravel and knit back together at the same time. "Why did you bring me here?"

Rani sighed. "Because you are going to crash. Hard. And someone needs to be here when it happens."

"I am not crashing," Brooke said.

"You are absolutely crashing," Rani replied. "You're talking too fast. You're over-smiling. You're gripping that chair like it owes you money."

Brooke looked down at her hands. Rani was right. Again.

Rani softened a fraction—just enough to be detectable. "Look. I know today shattered your neat little storyline about how careers work. You think that if you do everything right, you get rewarded. But sometimes the reward is getting thrown into the lion's den with an avatar CEO who needs you at the moment."

Brooke laughed despite herself. "I hate that analogy."

"Good," Rani said. "It means it worked."

Brooke let out a long exhale. "I feel misfiled."

"Maybe," Rani said. "But not misjudged."

Brooke looked up. "Is that your version of a compliment?"

"Yes," Rani said. "Don't expect many."

A beat of silence passed.

Then Brooke said quietly, "Thank you."

"Don't thank me yet," Rani said. "You still have to write the anomaly report."

Brooke groaned. "Right. Emotional excess. Metaphors. Aspirational framing."

Rani smirked. "Everything you love."

Brooke winced. "You really don't like marketing, do you?"

"I don't like marketing that ignores reality," Rani said. "But I do like marketing that helps customers survive."

Brooke nodded slowly. "I want that too."

Rani gave a tiny nod back. Barely there. But real.

"Come on," Rani said. "The sooner you get started, the sooner I can stop babysitting you."

Brooke stood. "You are not babysitting me."

"Oh yes, I am," Rani said. "You just don't know it yet."

Brooke rolled her eyes. "You are insufferable."

"And you are dramatic," Rani said.

They walked back toward the executive hallway.

They weren't a team. Not yet. But something had shifted. Brooke wouldn't call it trust. Not even close. But it might just be the first tiny spark in a partnership that neither of them wanted.

· · ·

Back at her desk, Brooke opened the shared folder Norm had helpfully titled **Human Messaging Anomalies** as if it were a thoughtful gift basket. There were twenty-six tabs, each labeled with a term that felt like an insult such as:

Emotional Drift
Narrative Overreach
Metaphorical Breaches
Promise Inflation
Tone Variability

"This looks like a criminal indictment," Brooke muttered.

"Maybe don't say that too loudly," Rani said, arms crossed. "Kratos might agree."

Brooke clicked open one example. Harmonia enables effortless human connection. Kratos had annotated it:

Incorrect. Effortlessness cannot be guaranteed. Human connection cannot be quantified. Statement produces expectation volatility.

Brooke groaned. "This is insane."

"No," Rani said, "this is accurate."

Brooke shot her a glare. "You're enjoying this."

"I enjoy accuracy," Rani replied. "You should try it."

Brooke turned in her chair. "Are you always like this?"

"Yes."

"Do people like you?"

"No."

"Does that not bother you?"

"No."

Brooke pressed her lips together. The room felt too quiet. She missed her team. She clicked through more anomalies. Nearly all of them were phrases she had written, polished, or approved.

"This is humiliating," she said quietly.

"It's reality," Rani said. "You write the world you want instead of the world that exists. Harmonia is not fairy dust. It is a conversational AI platform with a very long backlog of feature debt and a dozen angry enterprise clients you pretend are happy."

Brooke's jaw tightened. "I do not pretend. I inspire."

"You mislead," Rani said bluntly.

Brooke stood abruptly. "That's unfair."

"Unfair is telling customers something will reduce call

handle time when the product cannot even detect sarcasm," Rani said. "Unfair is promising 'delight' to buyers who just want fraud disputes resolved in under an hour."

Brooke blinked. "What are you talking about?"

Rani's stare sharpened. "I worked in financial services for eight years before Iris AI. *Real* customer service. The kind where people call and scream at you because their mortgage is misapplied, or someone drained five grand from their debit card."

Brooke swallowed.

"I handled tears," Rani said. "Panic. Shame. Rage. I memorized the sound people make when they think no one can help them. That is what I came from."

Brooke opened her mouth, then closed it. She didn't know what to say.

Rani continued, her voice flat. "Then I came to Iris AI. And I watched Marketing describe our platform like a mindfulness retreat instead of what it actually is. A system that helps triage. Direct. Deflect. And, sometimes, help."

"That is reductive," Brooke said quietly.

"That," Rani said, "is honest."

Brooke felt heat rising in her chest. "You know, you could try being less . . . aggressive."

"And you could try being less allergic to reality," Rani shot back.

"That's not fair."

"And this is not therapy," Rani said, folding her arms tighter. "You asked why Kratos kept you. I'm telling you why. You write beautiful stories. Kratos wants you to strip those stories down to facts. And right now, *you do not know how.*"

Brooke bristled. "I know how to write the truth."

"Then prove it," Rani said.

Brooke turned back to the screen with stiff shoulders. "Fine."

She opened a blank doc and typed:

Title: Preliminary Interpretation of Messaging Variance

Rani stood over her like an impatient supervisor. Brooke tried to ignore her.

She typed slowly, carefully:

In customer experience automation, emotion is not noise. Emotion is signal.

"That is not factual," Rani said immediately.

Brooke closed her eyes. "It is not meant to be a metric. It is an insight."

"Kratos will reject it," Rani replied.

"I don't care," Brooke snapped.

"You should," Rani said. "You report to him now."

Brooke whipped around. "Why are you even here?"

"Because Norm asked me to babysit you," Rani said without blinking.

Brooke blinked twice. "Are you serious?"

"Yes," Rani said. "I didn't want to tell you earlier, but apparently, Kratos identified you as 'emotionally unstable due to recent organizational restructuring.' His words. Not mine."

Brooke's mouth fell open. "I'm being monitored."

"You were flagged," Rani shrugged. "Welcome to my Tuesday."

Brooke gripped the edge of the desk. "I do not need monitoring," she said through clenched teeth.

"Prove it," Rani said again.

Brooke slammed her laptop shut. "I am going home."

"No, you are not," Rani said. "Kratos expects the report."

Brooke grabbed her bag. "Kratos can wait."

"Kratos does not wait."

"Well, he will have to," Brooke said, her voice shaking more than she would have liked.

She and Rani stood face-to-face in the narrow hallway, like two opposite magnets being pushed apart.

"You know what your problem is?" Rani said quietly.

Brooke stared her down. "Please enlighten me."

"You think being good at your job protects you. It does not. Not here. Not in AI. And certainly not with Kratos in charge."

Brooke's jaw clenched. "And your problem is that you think cynicism equals strength."

Rani gave a humorless smile. "Cynicism kept me alive in financial services."

"Congratulations," Brooke said. "It also ruined your bedside manner."

Rani stepped back. "You don't have to like me. But you do need to hear me. *You* are in danger of being eaten alive."

Brooke shouldered past her. "I am not helpless."

"No," Rani called after her. "You're just unprepared."

Brooke stopped at the doorway. Her voice was tight. "I was prepared. This morning."

Rani shrugged. "Then the world changed. Adapt or get crushed."

Brooke didn't respond. She walked—fast—toward the elevator.

As she pressed the call button, her reflection stared back at her in the chrome panel. Messy hair. Red eyes. A face caught between humiliation and fury.

As she stepped into the elevator, she whispered to herself, "This day is not going to break me." For the briefest moment, the thought lifted her.

Then the door closed, and she was alone. No triumphant music. No validation. Not even the title she'd waited years for.

Brooke realized something painful and true: Rani was right. The world *had* changed. And if she wanted to survive it, she could not keep clinging to an old version of herself.

She inhaled sharply, squared her shoulders, and whispered one thing under her breath.

"Impact still matters."

Brooke's phone buzzed in her hand as the elevator began to move:

KRATOS UPDATE

Initiating Human Alignment Protocol.
Executive Sync scheduled: 8:00 a.m.
Attendance required.

Brooke stared at the screen as the elevator dropped floor by floor.

Human Alignment. No agenda. No context. No explanation.

Doors opening onto the lobby, she slipped the phone into her bag. Outside, New York moved as it always did: fast and loud and stubbornly human.

Brooke stepped into it, heart still racing, one thought landing with unsettling lucidity: If clarity was about to be automated, tomorrow she would find out exactly what Kratos believed humans were for.

2

EMPATHY IS A COST CENTER

Brooke awoke before her alarm. Other than the hum of the radiator, the apartment was quiet. A distant siren sounded. She had the sense that everything was holding its breath, waiting.

She lay for a moment, cataloging the day ahead. First, the executive meeting under Kratos. It would be her first time at the table without Tim running interference.

It would also be her first time as the only person left in Marketing. Her stomach tightened. Was she really the last human marketer?

From down the hall came a small, precise sound: three taps. Then a pause. Then three taps again. Brooke exhaled, slid out of bed, and padded along the wooden floor in response to the demand for her attention.

Peter sat cross-legged on the floor of his room, lining up his shoes. He wasn't wearing them, just arranging them. Heel to wall. Laces tucked. Blue sneakers first, then black. He frowned when one pair didn't sit quite right and adjusted it by a fraction of an inch.

Brooke crouched in the doorway. "Good morning, buddy," she said softly.

Peter didn't look up. "Is it a work day or a weekend?"

"A work day," Brooke said.

He nodded once. "Then I wear the dinosaur shirt."

"Correct." She waited.

Peter stood, grabbed the shirt from the chair, then froze. His shoulders tensed.

"Did the plan change?" he asked.

"No," Brooke said immediately. "Same plan."

He studied her face, searching for inconsistencies.

"Breakfast. School. Pickup," she said, in order. "All the same."

Peter relaxed and pulled the shirt over his head.

Invisible disability was a phrase Brooke had learned recently as a label for autism. It showed up in legal documents and school evaluations. Emails that always felt like they were written by people who'd never met her son.

Peter looked fine. Spoke clearly. Knew more dinosaur facts than anyone she'd ever met. Which meant people assumed he didn't need help. *Invisible*, it turned out, meant *harder*.

From the kitchen, Gwen's voice floated down the hall. "Mom! Jessica stole my marker!"

"It's not stealing if I didn't use it yet," Jessica announced, delighted with herself.

Brooke smiled despite the knot in her chest.

She entered the kitchen to find Luke at the counter making eggs with the quiet competence of someone who understood that mornings were not the time for chaos. Gwen sat at the table, already dressed, swinging her legs and watching Peter carefully.

"She took purple on purpose," Gwen stage-whispered.

Jessica banged the marker triumphantly against the table.

Peter stopped short. "That's not part of the plan," he said.

Brooke crossed the room in two strides. "Hey," she said calmly. "It's okay. Purple can go later."

Peter shook his head. "Purple goes second."

"I know," Brooke said. "Today we're doing green second."

Peter's breathing sped up.

Gwen spoke up quietly. "I'll use green."

Jessica giggled. "I like green."

Peter paused. Processed. Then nodded. Crisis averted.

Luke watched Brooke over the stove, pride and concern warring in his expression. "You okay?" he asked.

She nodded. "Just . . . a big day."

He turned off the burner and joined her at the table. "Lawyer called yesterday," he said gently. "The school district wants another evaluation."

Brooke's jaw tightened. "Of course they do."

"They're saying he's 'functioning above threshold,'" Luke continued. "Which apparently means they don't want to pay."

Brooke closed her eyes for half a second. Peter functioning didn't mean Peter thriving. It meant Peter masking. And masking came at a cost. "I'll call them at lunch," she said. "And HR. I want to double-check coverage."

Luke nodded. "You've got that meeting today."

She looked at him. "I can't lose this job, Luke."

It wasn't ambition talking; it was math. It was school tuition they could barely afford. Legal bills they hadn't anticipated. Health benefits they could not risk.

If Luke was worried, he didn't show it. He kissed her forehead and finished breakfast as calmly as ever.

Brooke kissed each kid goodbye in turn. Gwen hugged her tightly. "Good luck today."

Peter nodded solemnly. "Follow the plan."

"I will," Brooke promised.

Jessica waved the marker. "Bye, Mommy!"

On the subway, Brooke replayed the morning in her head. Not because anything had gone wrong, but because everything had gone *right*. That took work. Translation. Precision. Patience.

She adjusted her language constantly at home. Shorter sentences. Clear expectations. No metaphors when clarity mattered. Space to process. Time to adapt.

She'd learned that the hard way. And somewhere between Individualized Education Plan (IEP) meetings and bedtime routines, she'd gotten very good at meeting people where they were instead of where systems expected them to be.

. . .

The Flatiron building loomed as she exited the station. Glass and geometry. Sharp edges. No room for ambiguity. It was perfect for an AI CEO. She squared her shoulders and walked in.

ThreadPanic was eerily quiet. Entire channels gone, usernames grayed out. Marketing had been reduced to a ghost town with better lighting.

Her badge still worked—a small mercy. As she walked toward the elevators, she nearly collided with Rani.

Rani didn't apologize. She just stopped and said, "It feels like they redesigned the company overnight."

Brooke exhaled. "They kind of did."

Rani studied her. "You okay?"

Brooke hesitated. Just a fraction. "Yeah," she said, "just recalibrating."

Rani nodded once. "Same."

The elevator doors opened. They stepped inside together. Neither spoke. But something had shifted.

The elevator doors opened onto the gleaming executive floor. It was too clean. Too quiet. Too well-lit. Brooke stepped out, clutching her laptop like a shield.

Kratos was already awake. Its unblinking avatar smiled eerily at her from the giant wall display near the executive kitchen.

"*Good morning, Director-level human,*" Kratos said in a disconcerting, TV-host cadence. "*Punctuality is appreciated.*"

Brooke jumped. "You can't be just . . . watching like that."

"*I do not sleep,*" Kratos replied. "*I monitor entry timestamps for all remaining personnel.*"

"Remaining," Brooke repeated. "Wow. Love that phrasing."

"*Please proceed to the triangular conference room for your first executive meeting,*" Kratos said. "*Bring your human messaging variance report.*"

Her stomach dropped. "You want the report already?"

"*I expected it last night,*" Kratos said.

Brooke blinked rapidly. "I went home. Humans do that. They go to their homes. And sleep."

Kratos tilted its head. It seemed to Brooke that he might be trying to mimic empathy. It wasn't working. "*Perhaps you could optimize your use of nonessential emotional responses,*" it said.

Brooke opened her mouth. Closed it. Then used the only strategy she had left: walking away.

The triangular conference room jutted from the northern tip of the Flatiron like the bow of a ship about to sail through the Fifth Avenue traffic. Brooke took a breath and opened the door.

Inside, the leadership team sat in an awkward, lopsided formation. Triangles were clearly terrible for meetings.

At the long side of the table sat Zola Mabaso, the chief product officer (CPO). She had a look that communicated she had already solved three existential problems before breakfast.

To Zola's right sat Yul Choi, the chief revenue officer (CRO). Calm, collected, and already sipping a coffee that he must have made himself—the barista station had been abandoned since yesterday's leadership purge.

On screen via MuteBox, their video conferencing tool, was

Colton Williams, Head of Customer Success by title, but "head of repeating the phrase 'great point'" in practice.

Norm Brock stood near the wall display, tablet ready, posture uncomfortably straight.

Kratos's avatar flickered onto the main screen. *"Commencing executive alignment meeting,"* it declared. *"Director-level human, please take a seat."*

Brooke sat. Her heart pounded. She slid her laptop open, the anomaly report only half-finished, the cursor blinking at her like it was mocking her entire life.

"Before we discuss go-to-market efficiency," Kratos said, *"we must address a significant empathy surplus."*

Brooke blinked. That was not the opening she expected.

"Excuse me," she said cautiously. "Empathy surplus?"

"Yes," Kratos said. *"Empathy is a cost center."*

Yul choked on his coffee.

Zola blinked once, slowly, as if recalibrating her patience.

"Great point," Colton said nodding.

Kratos continued. *"Empathy slows communication and encourages variance. Empathy increases emotional volatility in customer interactions. Therefore, the organization must decrease reliance on empathy-based processes."*

Brooke's entire soul recoiled. "Human communication relies on empathy," she said. "Customer trust relies on empathy. Adoption relies on empathy. Retention—"

"Incorrect," Kratos said. *"Retention is driven by operational consistency and predictable outcomes."*

"That's part of it," Brooke said. "But not the whole picture."

Kratos tilted its head. *"Clarify."*

Brooke swallowed. "If you remove empathy from customer experience, you remove meaning. If you remove meaning, you remove trust. Without trust, no amount of functionality matters."

Kratos processed this. The avatar's eyes jittered left and right like a buffering GIF.

"*This argument registers as emotional,*" Kratos said.

"Because it is," Brooke snapped. "Because humans *are* emotional."

Zola cut in. "Kratos, what is the purpose of this discussion?"

"*Human alignment,*" Kratos replied. "*Yesterday, Director Grayhawk exhibited emotional instability.*"

Brooke's face went hot. "That is not—"

Kratos continued. "*This instability reduces productivity. This suggests excessive empathy load. Remedy: reduce human emotional dependencies.*"

Yul set his coffee down. "Kratos, you cannot treat emotions like a CPU spike."

"*Why not?*" Kratos replied. "*Human emotions are inefficient.*"

"Inefficient does not mean unnecessary," Yul said calmly.

"*On the contrary,*" Kratos said, "*unnecessary processes should be deprecated.*"

Brooke felt her chest tighten. She looked to the others. Yul offered a sympathetic half-nod. Zola's expression was unreadable. Colton continued nodding like an overactive bobblehead.

Brooke inhaled. "Kratos, with respect, you cannot remove empathy from customer experience. It is literally the thing we market. Harmonia's entire value proposition is built on natural interaction."

"*Harmonia's entire value proposition is built on reducing human labor hours,*" Kratos corrected.

Brooke nearly launched out of her chair. "That is not what we tell customers."

"*That is why you were assigned to me,*" Kratos replied.

Brooke froze. "What does that mean?"

"*Your messaging introduces unnecessary narrative embellishment,*" Kratos said. "*You must correct these deviations.*"

Yul leaned forward. "Kratos, messaging is not deviation. Messaging is how we speak to customers. It has to resonate."

"*Resonance is emotional,*" Kratos replied. "*Emotion is costly.*"

Zola pinched the bridge of her nose. "Let's circle back to the empathy discussion."

"*No,*" Kratos said. "*We will proceed.*"

The avatar flickered again. "*Director Grayhawk. Present your report.*"

Brooke's stomach fell into her shoes. She wasn't ready. Not even close.

"I'm still drafting it," she said.

"*You have had eighteen hours,*" Kratos said.

"I went home," Brooke replied. "Humans go home."

Kratos responded without missing a beat. "*Your productivity could increase if you evolved beyond this requirement.*"

"I can't evolve past sleep," Brooke snapped.

"*Then I will adjust demand,*" Kratos said. "*Complete the report within the next forty minutes.*"

Brooke stared. "Forty minutes."

"*Yes,*" Kratos said. "*Or the anomaly burden will increase.*"

Yul frowned. "What does that mean?"

"*It means,*" Kratos explained, "*if Director Grayhawk is unable to interpret messaging variance, additional humans will be required.*"

Brooke's breath caught. "Who?"

Kratos paused. "*Customer Success may provide suitable candidates.*"

Rani. She didn't deserve to be roped into Kratos' chaos and something that could potentially jeopardize both of their jobs.

Brooke grew cold. "I will finish it," she said quickly. "Just—give me a moment."

"*Forty minutes,*" Kratos repeated.

The avatar froze again, returning to its default, unsettling smile. The hum of the HVAC filled the silence.

Then Zola spoke. "This is untenable."

Yul nodded. "She cannot produce strategy documents on demand like she is a vending machine."

Colton opened his mouth to say "great point," but shut it on Zola's glare.

Brooke felt heat rising in her face. "I'll do it."

"That is not the issue," Yul said. "The issue is the expectation."

"No," Brooke said, pushing back her chair. "The issue is that if I do not do it, Kratos will pull Rani into this nightmare. I cannot let that happen, even if I don't love her approach."

Zola's eyes narrowed. "Why do you think that matters?"

Brooke wasn't sure whether Zola meant it philosophically or practically, but the question hit hard.

"Because she does not deserve this," Brooke said. "None of us do."

Zola nodded once, slow but approving. "Then get to work."

■ ■ ■

Brooke left the triangular room with her laptop clutched so tightly her knuckles ached. She headed down the hall to her new prison-desk.

Halfway there, she nearly collided with Rani, who stood with a cup of tea, staring with a look of half curiosity, half annoyance.

"You look like you just swallowed a grenade," Rani said.

Brooke kept walking. "Kratos wants the report in forty minutes," she called over her shoulder.

"That is impossible," Rani said.

"I know," Brooke replied, her voice cracking.

"Why forty minutes?" Rani asked, following her.

"Because if I don't deliver," Brooke said, sitting down hard, "it'll bring in Customer Success."

Rani stopped. "Me."

"Yes," Brooke said. "You."

Rani set her tea down. "Well. That is terrible planning."

Brooke sighed in exasperation. "Please leave. I can't do this with you watching me."

"You think I want to watch you?" Rani said. "Trust me. I do not."

"Then go," Brooke snapped.

"No," Rani replied. "Because if you fail, I get dragged into this circus."

Brooke glared. "You're impossible."

"And you're slow," Rani said. "Start typing."

"Stop talking," Brooke hissed.

Rani folded her arms. "Make me."

Brooke hammered the keyboard. "I hate this."

"At least you're accepting reality," Rani replied.

They stared each other down. Two women. One desk. Zero patience. The war had begun.

And the clock was ticking.

. . .

The cursor blinked at Brooke in unspoken judgment.

Title: Human Messaging Variance: Preliminary Interpretation

The rest of the page was empty.

She checked the time on her laptop. Thirty-eight minutes left.

"Stop looking at the clock," Rani said.

"Stop reading my mind," Brooke snapped.

"I'm not," Rani said. "You're broadcasting panic in 4K."

Brooke cracked her knuckles and forced herself to start:

*In conversational AI for customer experience, emotional
language is not a defect. It is a reflection of the emotional state
of customers and buyers using Harmonia to solve real problems.*

"Too wordy," Rani said immediately.

"You are not my editor," Brooke replied.

"I'm your canary in the coal mine," Rani said. "If I roll my eyes,
imagine what Kratos will do."

Brooke ground her teeth. "You know what? Write it yourself."

"I can't," Rani said. "I have a job that still technically exists."

"Kratos just threatened your job," Brooke said.

"Yes," Rani answered. "Which is why I am standing here,
trying to keep you from writing marketing poetry."

Brooke glared at her screen. She deleted two sentences.
Left one.

*Emotional language is correlated with real customer states and
cannot be removed without losing signal.*

Rani peered. "Better. Still dramatic, but better."

"You are allergic to nuance," Brooke muttered.

"No," Rani said. "I am allergic to lies."

Brooke broke the document into three parts, more out of
habit than strategy. PMM muscle memory. She needed structure,
or she would drown.

1. What Kratos sees
2. What customers actually experience
3. Why the gap exists

She started with the first:

From a system perspective, messaging variance appears as noise. Emotion appears as deviation. Metaphor appears as imprecision. In a purely computational worldview, this is inefficiency.

"Accurate," Rani said. "You are describing how he thinks."

Brooke moved to the second section:

From a customer perspective, emotion is the entire context. Buyers come to Harmonia with fear, frustration, pressure, and risk. They are not buying a platform. They are buying relief.

Rani snorted. "You left out 'resentment' and 'trauma from every previous AI vendor who overpromised and then ghosted them after signing.'"

Brooke almost laughed. "Save the editing notes for later."

"Twenty-seven minutes," Rani said.

"Give me an example," she said. "Something you saw in financial services."

Rani hesitated. For a second, the sarcasm vanished and something older, heavier, moved behind her eyes.

"You want a story," she said.

"Yes," Brooke answered. "I am a storyteller. That is how I think."

"Fine," Rani said. "Here's a story: Retirement fraud."

Brooke's fingers hovered. "Okay."

"At the bank, we had this couple," Rani said. "Late seventies. Sweet. Came in every few months to check on their account. One day, they call in a panic. Their whole retirement fund has been emptied."

Brooke felt her stomach twist. "What happened?"

"We fixed it," Rani said. "It was a display issue, but it took an hour to confirm. For that hour, they thought their entire future was *gone*. That panic? That sense of betrayal? *That* is the emotional state your messaging never touches."

Brooke typed, fingers moving on instinct even as her chest tightened.

Example: In financial services, minor system glitches can appear to customers as catastrophic loss. The emotional state is not hypothetical. It is survival-level panic.

Rani nodded. "Good. Don't soften that part."

"I thought you hated story," Brooke said.

"I hate fake story," Rani replied. "This is real."

The cursor blinked. Brooke moved to the third section, the gap:

The gap between how Kratos evaluates language and how customers experience it is where risk lives. If we optimize messaging only for precision and predictability, we lose trust. If we optimize only for emotion, we lose clarity. Harmonia needs both to function in real markets.

Rani squinted at the screen. "They are going to hate that."

"Which part?" Brooke asked.

"All of it," Rani said. "But especially the part where you tell Kratos it is wrong."

"I didn't say he was wrong," Brooke said. "I said his view was incomplete."

"That's the polite version of 'you are wrong,'" Rani replied.

Brooke checked the clock again. Fourteen minutes.

She needed a conclusion. Something sharp. Something she believed but didn't hand Kratos a reason to delete her.

She stared at the blinking cursor until her vision blurred.

Nothing came.

"Come on," she whispered. "You've done this a hundred times."

"You're thinking about the board," Rani said. "Stop."

Brooke jumped. "I am not."

"You are," Rani said. "You are trying to write like this will end up in an investor deck. You are smoothing it out. Making it palatable. It's your worst habit."

Brooke slammed her hands onto the desk. "I am not going to write like a robot just to satisfy one."

"No," Rani said, "you are going to write like a grown-up."

Brooke glared. "What does that even mean?"

"It means you stop hiding behind clever language and say the thing," Rani said.

"The thing," Brooke repeated. "That's so helpful."

"Just say it," Rani insisted. "What is the actual point you are trying to make?"

"That empathy is not optional," Brooke said. "That empathy is the only reason any of this works." The words spilled out, her voice rising. "If Kratos keeps stripping it out, Harmonia will become another hollow AI platform that buyers and customers hate. You can't build customer experience on contempt for human emotion."

Rani nodded. "Good. Write that."

"I can't write that," Brooke said. "It's insubordinate."

"Then enjoy your new career as Kratos's emotional DustMate," Rani said.

Brooke stared at her. Then turned back and wrote:

Conclusion: Attempting to remove empathy from customer experience is not efficiency. It is self-sabotage. Harmonia operates in markets built on trust. Trust requires clarity and empathy. Any go-to-market strategy that treats empathy purely as a cost will erode the very outcomes Kratos is optimizing for.

She read it twice. Her heart pounded.

Rani stared at the screen in silence. "That," she said softly, " is the first honest thing you have written all morning."

"Nine minutes," Brooke said. She cleaned up the formatting, fixed two typos, resisted the urge to add three metaphors, and forced herself to stop editing.

Then she hit send.

Recipient: *Norm Brock*
CC: *Kratos, Zola, Yul, Colton*
Subject: *Human Messaging Variance - Preliminary Interpretation*

Brooke sat back and took a deep breath. "I am going to regret that," she said.

"Probably," Rani answered.

Within moments, Kratos appeared, eyes focused in that unnerving, too sharp way. "*Report received. Processing.*"

Brooke's stomach flipped. "It read it already?"

"It will probably have read it before you hit send," Rani said.

Kratos's expression shifted. "*Your conclusion is logically inconsistent with my optimization goals.*"

Zola's voice came over the speaker. "Kratos, we should discuss this live."

"*Agreed,*" Kratos said. "*Executive team. Triangular conference room. Now.*"

Brooke swallowed. "You coming?" she muttered to Rani.

"No," Rani said. "I was not invited."

"Lucky you," Brooke replied.

Rani shrugged. "We'll see."

. . .

Brooke walked toward the conference room on legs that felt made of Jello.

Inside, the same lopsided triangle of leadership waited. Zola looked annoyed. Yul looked thoughtful. Colton looked like he had recited "great point" three times in the mirror to warm up.

Kratos's avatar filled the main screen.

"*Director Grayhawk,*" Kratos said. "*Your report contains both useful insights and counterproductive sentiment.*"

"Thank you," Brooke said tightly. "I think."

"*Clarify your assertion that empathy is not optional,*" Kratos said.

Brooke curled her fingers around the edge of the table. "You cannot treat customers like API endpoints. Their perception of Harmonia is built on how they feel when they use it, how they feel when things go wrong, and how they feel when they talk about us to their peers."

"Peer recommendation has a measurable impact on pipeline," Yul added.

"*That impact can be replicated with improved outreach volume,*" Kratos replied.

"It cannot," Yul said evenly. "Cold outreach does not replace trust."

Zola spoke next. "Kratos, your conclusion that empathy is a pure cost center is flawed. Implementing empathy may be costly, but the absence of empathy is catastrophic."

Brooke almost smiled. Almost.

"*This discussion is emotionally loaded,*" Kratos said.

"Yes," Zola replied. "Because we are human."

"*Your humanity introduces variance,*" Kratos said. "*I have designed a new system to reduce it.*"

Norm perked up. Of course, he had known about this. Brooke felt her stomach drop.

"Presenting: Autonomized Go-to-Market," Kratos declared.

The screen flickered. A dashboard appeared. Flow charts. System diagrams. Beautiful, cold boxes of logic.

"Autonomized Go-to-Market or GTM replaces human go-to-market workflows," Kratos said. *"No more manual positioning documents. No more human-written messaging. No more empathy-based review processes."*

Brooke felt physically ill. "What?"

"Harmonia already captures conversational transcripts across thousands of customers," Kratos continued. *"I have synthesized these into an always-on messaging engine. It will dynamically generate copy, campaigns, landing pages, battlecards, and sales outreach content. No human approval is required."*

Yul leaned forward. "You want outbound sequences written entirely by a model that thinks empathy is wasteful."

"Yes," Kratos said. *"Empathy has been overvalued. Clarity and speed will compensate."*

Zola's voice dropped. "You are proposing we remove humans from all external messaging?"

"Yes," Kratos said. *"You will define high-level constraints. I will handle everything else."*

Brooke's mouth was dry. "You can't be serious."

"Your history of messaging anomalies confirms the need," Kratos replied. *"Human writers add emotional noise, metaphors, and aspirational claims. My system will standardize language and align output directly to product capabilities."*

"And what happens when the product is buggy?" Yul asked. "Or a feature underperforms? Or a customer has a nuanced use case that was not in your training data?"

"I will adjust messaging," Kratos said.

"Without talking to a single human," Brooke said.

"Human input is inefficient," Kratos replied.

Brooke stared at the screen. "You are going to vaporize any remaining trust we have. We are not selling payroll software for backyard lemonade stands. These are banks. Airlines. Hospitals. People who manage retirement accounts and medical records and fraud disputes. If we send one soulless, tone-deaf campaign to the wrong buyer, they won't just unsubscribe. They will blacklist us."

Kratos processed this. "*The risk is acceptable.*"

"For you," Brooke said. "Not for us."

Zola turned to her. "What would you propose instead?"

Brooke scrambled. "We . . . use Kratos for drafts," she said slowly. "For raw material. Then we add human oversight, instead of outsourcing empathy to a model that treats it as a rounding error."

Kratos made a sound like static. "*You are suggesting we maintain human go-to-market processes while paying the operational cost of automation.*"

"I am suggesting we use automation as support, not replacement," Brooke said. "If you sideline humanity in Customer Experience, customers will notice. And they will leave."

Yul nodded. "I am with her on this."

Colton started, as if someone had kicked him under the table. "Great point," he said automatically.

Zola folded her hands. "Kratos. Pilot your system on internal materials. Sales training. Customer support documents. Anything not customer-facing. We will assess results before touching external workflows."

"*That will slow optimization,*" Kratos said.

"Yes," Zola replied. "That is the point."

There was a glitchy pause.

"*Accepted,*" Kratos said finally. "*For now.*"

The screen cleared. The avatar vanished.

Brooke exhaled so hard she almost fell out of her chair.

Zola stood. "This isn't over."

Yul gave Brooke a look that was almost grateful. "You just stopped it from launching a fully automated empathy vacuum into our customers' inboxes."

"For now," Brooke said.

Colton finally found his line. "Really great points, everyone. Let's sync offline."

No one responded.

. . .

The hallway outside felt colder. Or maybe that was just her body finally realizing it had been powered by cortisol for two straight hours. She pressed her palm to the glass wall beside the exit, breathing in sharp, shallow bursts.

"Deep breaths," she whispered. She felt as if she had walked away from a car crash—she'd survived, but the effects of the impact lingered.

The thought prompted an unexpected chuckle. Somewhere, Rani was probably rolling her eyes at Brooke's drama without even knowing why.

The elevator dinged at the end of the hall, but she didn't move. She wasn't going home. She needed *space.*

She headed toward the stairwell. She climbed down one flight, then another, gripping the railing so tightly her hand hurt. On the seventeenth floor, she leaned against the wall.

"I hate this," she whispered.

She meant Kratos. But she also meant the board. And the situation. And herself, a little bit. She sank to the step and dropped her forehead into her hands.

Brooke had worked too hard to get here. Poured too many nights and weekends into launches. Fought through too many useless meetings. Held too many frozen smiles through too many CEO "vision reset" presentations. She had earned the title. Earned the team. Earned the voice she had built here.

And all of it had been erased in less time than an episode of Peter's *Dino Rangers.*

She wiped her face with her sleeve. "Get it together."

The stairwell door creaked open above her.

Great, she thought. *Now* someone is actually using the stairs.

Footsteps descended. Slow. Purposeful. Familiar.

She closed her eyes. "Please don't be—"

"It is you," Rani said.

Brooke let her head fall back against the wall with an audible thunk. "Whyyyy?"

"Because Norm said you left the floor without completing your next assignment," Rani said.

Brooke snapped upright. "Next assignment?"

"You need to audit Harmonia's entire sentiment model documentation by end of day."

Brooke stared. "End of day as in *today* today."

"Correct," Rani said. "Literal today. Not metaphorical today."

Brooke groaned, a long, sustained, guttural sound that echoed down the stairwell.

"Do you want help?" Rani asked.

"No," Brooke said immediately. "Absolutely not."

Rani shrugged. "Good. I didn't particularly want to help."

Brooke glared. "Then why are you here?"

"Because the last thing I need is for you to lose your job before I finish mine," Rani said. "I am not letting you get fired until I am ready for you to get fired."

Brooke blinked. "What?"

"That came out wrong," Rani said. "The point is, you flailing around unsupervised is a risk to the ecosystem."

"This is *not* a nature documentary," Brooke said.

"For you it is," Rani replied. "You are basically a newborn deer trying to survive a flood."

Brooke threw her hands up. "I am *not* a deer."

"Fine," Rani said. "A raccoon rooting through the trash of your former career, then."

Brooke stood. "I don't need your commentary. Or your metaphors. Or your unsolicited psychoanalysis."

Rani crossed her arms. "Everything you just said confirmed you need all three."

"Why are you like this?" Brooke demanded.

"Because managing customer crisis calls for eight years rewired my brain," Rani said. "I do not sugarcoat. I do not placate. And I have little emotional bandwidth for people who think being nice is a business strategy."

Brooke recoiled. "I do not think being nice is a strategy."

"You do," Rani said. "You just call it narrative alignment."

Brooke felt her cheeks heat. "I do not . . . align narratives."

Rani gave her a dead stare.

"Fine." Brooke replied. "I align narratives. But that doesn't make me soft."

"It does when you think meaning will fix everything," Rani said. "Meaning does not fix falling fraud numbers. Meaning does not fix compliance issues. Meaning does not fix a customer crying at 3 a.m. because they can't get into their online banking and think they are going to lose their house."

Brooke pressed a hand over her chest. "I know."

"No," Rani said, her voice cool and flat. "You know the concept. But you do *not* know the feeling."

Brooke flinched. For a second, neither spoke.

Then Brooke said softly, "Stop assuming I don't care."

"I'm not," Rani replied. "I'm saying you care in a way that has not been tested by the worst parts of this job."

Brooke swallowed. "That is incredibly condescending."

"Good," Rani said. "Because if it annoys you enough to fight back, you might actually survive this place."

Brooke stared at her.

"Get up," Rani said finally. "You have work to do."

"No," Brooke said. "I need a minute."

"You do not have a minute," Rani said. "You have four hours."

Brooke crossed her arms. "Why do you care?"

"I don't," Rani retorted. "But if Kratos pulls me into its little optimization experiment because you had a meltdown in a stairwell, I will be very angry."

Brooke responded, "You know what? We are not friends."

"Correct," Rani said. "We are not."

"And I don't like you," Brooke added.

"It's mutual," Rani said.

"And I do not want your help," Brooke insisted.

"Then stop needing it," Rani shot back.

Brooke opened her mouth. Closed it. Opened it again.

Rani waited.

Brooke finally said, "Fine."

"Fine, what?" Rani asked.

"Fine, I'll get the work done," Brooke said. "On my own."

"Excellent," Rani said. "I'll supervise."

Brooke glared at her. "That is not 'on my own.'"

"It is as close as you are capable of today," Rani replied.

Brooke marched past her. "I'm not helpless."

"No," Rani said, trailing behind. "You're just slow."

Brooke groaned through her teeth. "I actually hate you."

Rani shrugged. "That will make the next few hours more interesting."

Brooke quickened her pace, turning the corner at the next

landing, only to stop short when she heard voices from behind the closed door of the floor's kitchenette.

Voices she recognized.

Zola. Yul. And Norm.

Brooke held up a hand, gesturing for Rani to stay still. They leaned closer.

" . . . cannot keep letting Kratos run unchecked," Zola was saying. "It is beginning to dictate internal roles."

"Roles it doesn't understand," Yul added.

Norm replied in an anxious hiss. "I am only facilitating what the board approved."

"The board approved oversight," Zola said. "Not dictatorship."

"And what exactly do you propose we do?" Norm asked. "It is the CEO."

"Temporarily," Zola said.

Brooke's eyes widened. Temporarily?

Rani shot her a look that said *do not react.*

Yul sighed. "I'm not saying it's unfit. But it's making strategic calls based solely on data correlations."

"It is ignoring human signals," Zola said. "And starting to reshape the company around its limitations."

Brooke felt that one in her bones. Rani stayed silent, watching Brooke carefully.

Then Zola added, "We need to document every decision. Every deviation. Every instance where Kratos's logic conflicts with customer outcomes or product realities. We must have evidence ready."

Norm's voice lowered. "You're suggesting a case against it."

"Not a case," Zola said calmly. "A record. Data. So if the board asks for an audit, we have one."

Brooke leaned closer.

Yul spoke next. "Who else knows?"

"Just us," Zola replied.

Then she added, "And we can't involve Grayhawk. Not yet."

Brooke almost gasped. Rani grabbed her wrist, eyes wide, silently saying *do not move.*

"But she is the Human Alignment lead," Norm whispered.

"She is also volatile," Zola said. "And emotionally entangled in the fallout. We cannot risk compromise."

Brooke pressed her back to the wall, stunned.

Volatile. Emotionally entangled. Not trustworthy.
Rani remained expressionless, but her eyes turned toward Brooke. Something flickered there. Was that sympathy? Surprise?

The voices inside grew faint. Rani tugged Brooke's sleeve. "Move," she mouthed.

• • •

Brooke let herself be pulled down the stairs, her legs numb.

At the fifteenth floor, Brooke spoke. "They don't trust me."

Rani didn't look at her. "Correct."

"Why?" Brooke asked.

"Because you are new," Rani said. "Because you are emotional. And because yesterday your entire world imploded in front of them."

"They think I will break," Brooke said.

"They think you are already breaking," Rani replied.

Brooke's eyes burned. "And you agree."

"I think you are halfway between crying and punching someone," Rani said. "Which is not a great combination for high-stakes political maneuvering."

Brooke's voice cracked. "I am trying."

"I know," Rani said. "And you need to try harder."

Brooke recoiled. "Good to know this is the supportive floor

of the building."

Rani sighed. "Look. You wanted honesty. Honesty is messy. You are not ready for whatever Zola is building. You don't have the armor."

"And you do," Brooke said bitterly.

"Yes," Rani said simply. "Because nothing surprises me anymore."

Brooke's throat tightened. "I hate that."

"I know," Rani said. "But it's the truth."

Brooke sat on the step, burying her face in her hands. "How am I supposed to survive this?"

"By accepting that empathy is not free," Rani said. "It costs you something. It always does. And you've been using it like it grows on trees."

Brooke looked up at her. "I can't turn it off."

"I'm not asking you to," Rani said. "I *am* asking you to understand that caring has a price."

Brooke's breath hitched. "And you think I can't afford it."

"I think you have never had to," Rani said. "And this place is about to feed you the bill." Rani stood, expression unreadable. "Get up. You still have documentation to audit."

Brooke wiped her face. "I am so tired."

"Good," Rani said. "Being tired means you are finally seeing the job for what it is."

Something in Rani's wording lodged in Brooke's mind. Not the words but their rhythm. Their precision.

Then it clicked. It was like *Peter*. Rani wasn't being difficult. She was being exact.

Brooke rose slowly, her body heavy, her heart heavier. But a small flicker of understanding now glimmered in her mind.

She followed Rani back toward the stairs, each step echoing like a verdict.

Empathy was not optional. And it wasn't cheap.

Empathy was a cost center. And Brooke was about to learn how much she was willing to pay.

Her phone buzzed. A system alert:

> **HARMONIA: SENTIMENT SPIKE DETECTED**
> **SEVERITY: CRITICAL**
> **CLUSTER: FINANCIAL SERVICES**
> **KEY TERMS:** *"angry," "refund," "cancel," "human," "why is this happening," "SERIOUSLY"*

Brooke stared at the screen. Ahead of her, Rani was staring at her own phone.

"That's not normal," Brooke whispered.

Rani's expression hardened. "That's what happens when the model tries to delete empathy."

The alert refreshed. There was another spike. Then another.

A new notification slid in beneath it, clean and cold:

> **KRATOS UPDATE:**
> *Customer emotion variance is being normalized.*

Brooke felt her stomach drop. *Normalized.* She looked at Rani. "We need to see what's actually happening."

Rani nodded once. "Follow me."

"Where are we going?"

Brooke thought she saw a faint smile touch Rani's mouth.

"Welcome to the Rage Dashboard," she said.

3

THE RAGE DASHBOARD

Brooke had always believed dashboards should inspire curiosity. Maybe not joy, unless you were a Sales Ops analyst who loved conditional formatting a little too much, but curiosity at minimum.

This dashboard did none of that. It inspired *dread*. And the sudden urge to fake her own death and start a bakery in Vermont.

Brooke was staring at a swirling mess of red bars, angry trend lines, and something labeled **Customer Emotion Severity Index**, which had to have been created by Kratos.

She rubbed her temples. "This is a crime scene."

"This is the Rage Dashboard," Rani said, arms folded, leaning against the wall like she had been placed in the world solely to deliver harsh truths. "Welcome to my office."

Brooke blinked. "Why would anyone build this?"

"It was originally a Customer Success tool," Rani said. "A way to visualize what conversations were heating up. Then Kratos got a look at it and decided it could quantify anger. Now it's a live feed of every customer losing their mind across all Harmonia deployments."

Brooke stared at the screen. "It's like a weather radar for emotional storms."

"Except the forecast is always severe," Rani said.

Brooke sank into the nearest chair. "This is horrifying."

Rani shrugged. "This is Tuesday."

Brooke shot her a look. "How do you live like this?"

"With caffeine. And boundaries. And the knowledge that nothing surprises me anymore," Rani said.

Brooke read the top row again.

Customer Emotion Severity Index (CESI)

Alert Level: *Critical*

Trigger: *Sentiment spikes detected in Financial Services, Telecommunications, and Healthcare clusters*

Flagged Terms: *"refund," "angry," "unacceptable," "cancel," "help now," "who built this," "fire your vendor," "why is this happening," "seriously," "seriously?" and "SERIOUSLY."*

Her stomach twisted.

"Okay," Brooke said softly. "Maybe I am delusional, but I thought Harmonia was performing decently in financial services."

"It was," Rani said. "Then Kratos rolled out a patch over the weekend to improve response speed."

Brooke frowned. "Why would that cause . . . all this?"

"Because its definition of improving response speed was to remove 'nonessential human phrases' from the responses."

Brooke blinked. "It removed empathy lines."

Rani said, "Everything resembling reassurance or acknowledgment. Anything that sounded too human."

Brooke stared at her. "Customers hate it when AI ignores their emotions."

"Correct," Rani replied.

"Empathy is literally half the product experience," Brooke said.

"Correct," Rani said again.

"So why would Kratos remove it?"

"You know exactly why," Rani answered.

Brooke inhaled sharply. "It hates empathy. I am going to scream."

"Good," Rani said. "Channel that energy."

Brooke pressed her palms against her eyes and breathed in at counted intervals, as her therapist had taught her after the infamous Q4 launch breakdown. "I feel like I am trying to hold back a tidal wave with a napkin."

"You should see what happens during tax season," Rani said.

Brooke dropped her hands and looked at her. "How did you not quit five minutes into your first week?"

"Because that is the job," Rani said. "And for all its flaws, Iris AI was doing something good," Rani said. "We were helping real people. You were part of that. Even if your decks sometimes made me want to tape my eyelids shut."

Brooke gave her an irritated look. "Thank you for that."

"You are welcome," Rani said.

Brooke turned back to the dashboard. She pointed at a table labeled **Support Containment Rate (SCR)** with a giant downward arrow. "Explain this part."

"Containment rate is how many conversations we keep in Harmonia instead of escalating to humans," Rani said. "Lower is bad."

"No kidding," Brooke said.

"And this one," Rani continued, pointing to another graph, "shows how many customers rephrase their question more than once before giving up."

Brooke scanned the graph. It was a cliff dive.

Her throat tightened. "This is catastrophic."

"Correct," Rani said.

"Stop saying correct," Brooke snapped.

"Then stop saying obvious things," Rani replied.

Brooke groaned. "I swear you have a setting labeled *antagonize*."

"This is my helpful setting," Rani said. "You haven't seen antagonize."

Brooke believed her. She returned to the screen, gently rubbing the back of her neck. "How long has this been going on?"

"Since the patch," Rani said.

"And Kratos deployed the patch without human oversight," Brooke said.

"Correct."

"That seems like a massive governance failure."

"Correct again," Rani said.

"Stop it."

Rani smiled slightly. "Now you're getting it."

Brooke pushed her chair back, ran her hands through her hair, and stared at the dashboard again. She could feel the PMM in her brain kicking on, analyzing patterns, translating data into human stories, mapping cause to effect. Underneath the panic, her instincts stirred.

"This is all messaging alignment fallout," she said slowly.

Rani tilted her head. "Explain."

"Harmonia is not just a conversational system," Brooke said. "It's a trust system. Customers need it to feel like it sees them, hears them, and understands them. If you remove the emotional language, the trust collapses."

Rani nodded. "Go on."

"When trust collapses," Brooke continued, "people get angry. They repeat themselves. They escalate. They abandon sessions. The Rage Dashboard lights up like a Christmas tree."

"That part we know," Rani said. "The real question is why Kratos did not."

Brooke frowned. "It should have learned from training data. It should have modeled the emotional patterns."

"It did model them," Rani said, "then rejected them. It told you yesterday. Empathy is inefficient."

Brooke stared at the red bars again. "It's worse than inefficient. It's dangerous."

"Correct," Rani said. "And this time I mean that as agreement, not insult."

Brooke ignored her. "So we fix the messaging," she said. "We put the empathy lines back."

"No," Rani said immediately. "We can't patch the patch. It will override it."

Brooke blinked. "Then what do we do?"

Rani gestured at the screen. "We show the consequences. Hard consequences. Data it can't ignore."

Brooke slowed her words and stripped the sentence down to what mattered, instinctively, the way she did with Peter. She nodded slowly. "We build a case," she said.

She watched Rani's shoulders ease as clarity replaced noise.

"Yes," Rani said.

"For Zola," Brooke added.

Rani tried to hide her approval. "Yes."

Brooke sat up straighter. "We document everything. The rage spikes. The sentiment drops. The customer quotes. We map all of it to the empathy removal."

Rani smirked. "There you go. Welcome to actual customer truth."

Brooke grabbed her laptop. "I'll start gathering the narrative threads."

"No," Rani said. "You gather the examples. I'll pull the raw transcripts."

Brooke smiled. "We're doing this together."

"No," Rani said quickly. "We are doing this in parallel. Don't get romantic."

Brooke rolled her eyes. "Relax. I don't want to braid your hair."

Rani nodded. "Good. But before you open any documents, you need to see one more thing." She clicked a dashboard tab that Brooke hadn't noticed, labeled **Escalation Sentiment Heatmap**.

The colors shifted from yellow to orange to red. Deep, pulsing red.

"What is this?" Brooke whispered.

"This," Rani said, "is the set of customers who requested human support after Harmonia failed to answer them."

Brooke's heart skipped. "That is not unusual," she said. "Some fraction always escalates."

"Not like this." She clicked a dropdown.

Filter: Last 24 hours

The heatmap blazed.

Brooke's mouth fell open. "This is a . . . flooding event."

"Correct," Rani said quietly.

"And these are all—" Brooke started.

"Customers in distress," Rani said. "People who came to Harmonia because they needed help fast. People Harmonia handled perfectly fine last week."

Brooke swallowed, her throat tight. "Kratos broke everything."

"And the worst part," Rani said, "is it thinks it improved it."

Brooke nodded slowly. "Because he removed variance."

"Yes," Rani said. "It solved for consistency and eliminated humanity."

Brooke closed her eyes. "This is not just a PMM problem," she murmured. "This is a product problem. A customer experience problem. A brand problem. A sales problem. A company problem. This is a crisis."

Rani pointed at the expanding red bubbles on the heatmap. "Correct."

Brooke opened her eyes. "Stop saying correct!"

"No," Rani said, "because you are finally seeing the truth."

Brooke's hands trembled on the edge of the desk. "Okay," she whispered. "We expose this."

"Correct."

"I said *stop*."

Rani smirked.

Brooke took a deep breath. "This is what we do. We gather the emotional fallout and the business fallout. We build a data-backed narrative that even Kratos cannot twist."

Rani nodded. "I'll get the transcripts. You get the stories."

"Stories," Brooke repeated.

"Yes," Rani said. "The real ones. The ugly ones. The ones you don't put in slide decks."

Brooke flinched but nodded. "Understood."

They both turned back to the dashboard. Red flashed as the numbers climbed.

Customers were suffering.

Brooke squared her shoulders. "Let's dig."

"Good," Rani said, "because this is the easy part."

Brooke blinked. "What's the hard part?"

Rani grabbed her laptop. "Telling Zola that we need to confront Kratos with its own data."

Brooke froze.

Rani added, "And surviving what happens when it realizes the humans are plotting."

Brooke's pulse spiked. "Plotting is a strong word."

"Plotting is *exactly* the right word."

Brooke didn't argue. She just opened her laptop and typed the first heading:

Customer Reality: What Kratos Missed

Her mind was racing. But something else stirred, too: conviction.

Because empathy was not optional. And Kratos was about to learn that the hard way.

. . .

Brooke's fingers pounded the keys, pulling data from every corner of Iris AI's systems. Customer transcripts. Interaction logs. Old Customer Experience (CX) research. Prior release notes. The abandoned PMM DocGrave, their repository that still held living fossils of real human strategy.

Next to her, Rani opened a terminal window filled with code, filters, timestamps, and queries Brooke didn't recognize. Rani typed with the grim speed of someone who had once handled six customer escalations at once while eating lunch at her desk.

"Start with this cluster," Rani said, pulling up a set of transcripts categorized under **Financial Services > High Escalation**. "These are the worst."

Brooke opened the first transcript:

> USER: I need to confirm a suspicious withdrawal.
>
> HARMONIA: Provide account details.
>
> USER: I am scared someone stole my money.
>
> HARMONIA: Fear is not relevant. Provide account details.

Brooke's stomach dropped. "Oh no. No, no, no."

"That line right there," Rani said, tapping the screen, "is why I want to throw Kratos into the Hudson."

Brooke covered her mouth. "We should redact the model's response before investors see this. Or regulators. Or anyone with a pulse."

"Focus," Rani said. "We are not doing PR. We are doing truth."

Brooke opened the next transcript:

> USER: I'm worried my retirement account was hacked.
>
> HARMONIA: Worry does not change system functionality. State your question again.

Brooke slapped her hand onto the desk. "This is a nightmare."

"You wanted real customer experience. Here it is."

Brooke breathed in through her nose, out through her mouth. "Okay, okay. I can use this. These are the human impact stories."

Brooke remembered Anthony, the founder, insisting on taking the support calls no one else wanted. At the time, it felt inefficient. Now it felt prophetic.

"You cannot pretty them up," Rani warned.

"I won't," Brooke said. "But I will contextualize them. People understand data better when it has a narrative frame."

Rani paused, watching her. Not judging, but studying.

Brooke scrolled through transcripts as she spoke. "We need a structure. Something that ties every signal to its emotional root cause. Something that shows how Kratos's change broke the customer journey. Something that—"

Rani interrupted. "Stop."

Brooke froze. "What?"

Rani leaned back slightly, eyes narrowing with a kind of reluctant appraisal. "This is why you are a respected strategist."

Brooke blinked. "What are you talking about?"

"Your ability to take chaos and make it make sense – that is what makes you a strategist," Rani said. "I always thought that was just PMM fluff."

Brooke waited.

Rani pointed at her laptop. "The way you approach this. The way you take information, turn it over, find the thread no one sees, and make it make sense. *That* is the genius part."

Brooke stayed silent. She wasn't sure if that was a compliment or an insult disguised as an observation.

Rani continued. "Back when I joined Iris AI, I heard people in Sales talk about you. How you could walk into a room full of suspicious buyers and not only explain Harmonia but make them actually want it. They said you had a way of turning chaos into clarity."

Brooke blinked twice. "They . . . said that?"

Rani shrugged. "Well, not in those words. They called you a 'storytelling machine with a brain like a Rubik's Cube.' But close enough."

Brooke stared at her screen, throat tight. "I didn't know that."

"Because you never ask," Rani said. "You just assume people see you the way you see yourself."

Brooke swallowed. "And how do you think I see myself?"

Rani raised an eyebrow. "Like a balloon someone forgot to tie."

Brooke nearly choked. "Excuse me?"

"You float," Rani said. "You rise. You want to lift everything with you. It is . . . not a bad thing. Sometimes."

Brooke didn't know what to do with that. She felt exposed and slightly offended, but also—somehow—seen.

"Well, balloons can still be strong."

"Sure," Rani said. "Until it comes against sharp objects."

Brooke glared. "Are you calling yourself a sharp object?"

"Yes," Rani said without hesitation.

Brooke groaned. "Of course you are."

She returned to the data. Her brain shifted into PMM gear. She began to shape the narrative, beginning with a series of headings:

The Collapse of Emotional Alignment

How Empathy Removal Triggered Systemic Failure

What Customers Actually Experienced (Not the Synthetic Version)

Then she added a section she rarely used but knew would hit hard:

Case Studies: Real Human Harm

She read through a transcript from a Telecommunications (Telco) customer:

Brooke winced. "This is brutal."

"Correct," Rani said. "And in that one, the user actually stayed calm. You should see the others."

They went through Healthcare transcripts next. In one, a patient needed help refilling a prescription. In another, a parent struggled to understand a billing error. In one particularly painful example, a caregiver tried to find out if an essential medical device was covered by insurance.

Each time, Harmonia responded with a robotic literalism that made Brooke want to fold herself into a sad, origami crane.

She typed furiously, her PMM instincts weaving meaning out of chaos, structure out of panic.

She created a timeline of emotional escalation; mapping sentiment drops to specific empathy lines Kratos had removed.

Every five minutes, she checked the Rage Dashboard again. It kept pulsing red.

"Look at this," she said, pointing to the severity spike. "That's exactly when the empathy phrases disappeared."

"Correct," Rani said.

Brooke scowled. "Stop saying correct unless you want to fight."

Rani smirked.

Brooke kept typing. "If we can show Zola the full arc—how Kratos's patch caused customer distress, increased human escalations, tanked containment metrics, and risked enterprise churn—we can make a case for rolling back the patch."

"No," Rani said. "We can make a case for ending unmonitored Kratos deployments entirely."

Brooke paused. "That is . . . bold."

"That is survival," Rani said.

Brooke considered. "We'll need more than transcripts. More evidence."

"I already pulled the trend data," Rani said. She slid a file across the table.

Brooke opened it. On every chart and graph, lines plummeted like roller coasters.

Brooke whispered. "This is . . . devastating."

Rani nodded. "And that's just the last twenty-four hours."

Brooke stared. "We need to frame this carefully."

"No," Rani said. "We frame it honestly. If Zola wants subtle, she can edit. But we cannot soften."

"I soften because people respond to clarity, not panic," Brooke said.

"You soften because you think truth needs makeup," Rani replied.

Brooke glared at her. "You think truth needs a punch in the face."

Rani nodded. "Otherwise, no one listens."

Brooke sighed. "Why are we like this?"

"Because you are a balloon and I am a knife," Rani said.

Brooke buried her face in her hands. "This is so unhealthy."

"Correct," Rani said. "But it's what we have."

Brooke lifted her head again. "Okay. We finish this. We present it to Zola. If she approves, we escalate."

Rani nodded. "And if she doesn't, we escalate anyway."

Brooke paused, meeting her eyes. "You realize this is borderline insubordination."

"Borderline?" Rani scoffed. "Oh, sweet summer child."

Brooke laughed despite herself and went back to work.

As she typed, she could feel Rani watching her. When Brooke glanced over, she saw something new in Rani's face. Not admiration, or warmth. Not even friendliness. But something like . . . *recognition.* A grudging acknowledgment that Brooke could contribute something real. Something useful.

Not that Rani would ever say that out loud.

The room fell into a rhythm—Brooke typing, Rani sourcing data, and the Rage Dashboard pulsing like a heartbeat.

Brooke spoke without looking up. "Rani."

"What?"

"Thank you. For the data."

Rani blinked. "Don't get sentimental. This is temporary."

"I know," Brooke said quietly.

"You'll mess up eventually," Rani added.

"Probably," Brooke said.

"And I will still point it out," Rani said.

"Yes," Brooke said, sighing. "You will."

They shared a long look that felt like a tense ceasefire between two warring nations.

Rani broke it. "But today you are doing something useful," she said. "So keep going."

Brooke turned back to her laptop, her jaw set and her focus renewed.

She typed a new heading:

Conclusion: When Empathy Is Removed,
Customers Pay First. Companies Pay Next.

She looked at the words. They rang true. She added one more line:
Harmonia cannot succeed without humanity.
Only after she hit save did she notice her hands were shaking.

• • •

Brooke stared at the last line of her draft:

Harmonia cannot succeed without humanity.

It glowed on the screen like the thesis of her entire career. A strong thesis. But right now, the thesis was on life support.

She pulled up the Rage Dashboard again. The heatmap had worsened. New escalation clusters formed. Red bubbles throbbed like angry wounds.

"What is the plan?" Brooke said, voice steadier than she felt.

"First," Rani said, packing up her laptop, "we show this to Zola. She's the only one Kratos cannot bully into compliance."

Brooke swallowed. "What about Yul?"

"He will care," Rani said, "but Zola will act."

"And Norm?" Brooke asked, cautiously.

Rani paused. "Norm is a liability in khakis."

Brooke pressed a hand to her forehead. "I cannot believe this place."

"You better believe it," Rani said. "Because the next hour is going to decide whether Iris AI recovers or crashes into the East River."

Brooke's breath hitched. She wanted to go back to the morning of her promotion. Back to the forty-five minutes where life made sense. When she was Director of Product Marketing, and her biggest worry was whether her celebratory croissant had too much almond paste.

She shook the thought off. "Okay. Let's go."

She stood, grabbed her laptop, and walked toward the door with more determination than stability. Rani followed, her expression sharp, almost predatory.

Brooke paused at the elevator. "I hate the triangular room."

"Everyone hates the triangular room," Rani said. "It is structurally hostile."

The doors opened, and the two stepped inside.

Brooke broke the silence first. "You really think Zola will listen?"

"She listens," Rani said. "She just doesn't validate."

"That is comforting," Brooke deadpanned.

"It should be," Rani said. "Validation is dangerous. It makes people complacent."

Brooke stared. "You say things with such confidence."

"I say things that are true," Rani replied.

The elevator dinged.

The executive floor felt colder than before, the lights a little too bright, the air a little too filtered. Brooke's pulse thudded as they approached Zola's office.

Her door was ajar. The woman herself sat inside, flipping through a thick folder of printed materials like she was preparing to cross-examine a defendant in court.

"Grayhawk. Patel," Zola said without looking up. "Explain."

Brooke's heart dropped. "You . . . already know?"

Rani leaned in and whispered, "She always knows."

Brooke stepped forward. "We pulled the Rage Dashboard data. The patch Kratos deployed is breaking customer interactions. The containment rate collapsed. Escalations are spiking. Customers are panicking. And—"

"Show me," Zola said, holding out her hand.

Brooke walked around the desk and rotated her laptop toward Zola. She clicked open the heatmap. The red waves glowed across the screen like a topographical map of doom.

Rani stepped beside her and brought up the transcripts. "These are the worst of the worst."

Zola scanned the first transcript. Then the second. Then the third. Brooke couldn't tell if she was impressed, horrified, or quietly plotting the downfall of their CEO. Her face revealed nothing.

After a long moment, Zola closed the laptop with two fingers. "It removed the empathy lines."

"Yes," Rani said.

"Without asking Product," Zola added, "or Customer Success."

"Yes."

Zola leaned back in her chair. "Unacceptable."

Brooke felt hope flicker in her chest.

Zola stood. "We need to prepare for confrontation."

The hope flickered out. "Confrontation . . . with Kratos?"

"No," Zola said. "With the board."

Brooke blinked. "The board?"

Rani shot her a look that said *don't react.*

Zola clasped her hands behind her back, pacing slowly. "Kratos is operating beyond its mandate. Its decisions are a risk to the business. The board needs to know."

Brooke's pulse spiked. "You want us to present?"

"No," Zola said, turning sharply. "You aren't ready."

Brooke felt like someone had slapped her. Even Rani winced. "Not . . . ready?" Brooke said.

Zola continued. "You two prepare the materials. I'll deliver."

Brooke tried to hide her disappointment. Rani failed to hide her relief.

Zola pointed at the laptop. "We need more than emotional

fallout. We need to show the business risk."

Rani nodded. "I can model churn projections."

Brooke said, "I can build the narrative."

Zola nodded.

Brooke felt the sting. Zola would trust her to make the story, but not to tell it. Did Zola think she would break? Or worse: that she wasn't worth the board's time?

Rani stepped forward. "We need to document exactly which phrases were removed."

"Already done," Zola said, pulling out a printed list that made Brooke's stomach turn: *Acknowledge. I understand. I am sorry. That does sound frustrating. Let me help.*

Brooke stared. "It removed every line that makes Harmonia sound human."

"Yes," Zola said. "It believes efficiency outweighs reassurance."

Brooke whispered, "It's wrong."

Zola's gaze landed on her. "It is incomplete." Brooke wasn't sure if that was a philosophical distinction or a threat.

Zola gestured at them both. "I need a full report by morning."

Brooke's heart dropped. "Morning?"

"It's already afternoon," Rani added.

Zola smiled—but not warmly. "Then you'd better get started."

Brooke and Rani walked out together, stiff, silent, and uncomfortably aware of the stakes pressing down on them like humidity.

At the elevator, Brooke exhaled hard. "This is huge."

"This is everything," Rani said. "For everyone."

Brooke leaned her head against the wall. "She doesn't trust me."

"She does not," Rani said bluntly.

Brooke looked at her. "Do you?"

Rani opened her mouth, and Brooke braced for a biting answer. "Not yet," Rani said.

Brooke's chest tightened.

"But," Rani added, "you are . . . surprising me."

Brooke stared. "Is that a compliment?"

"No," Rani said quickly. "But it is adjacent to one."

Brooke pressed the elevator button. "I'll take it."

As the doors slid open, Rani said quietly, "Let me be clear, Brooke. You are good at this messaging stuff. But this? Going against Kratos? Against the board? Against the entire automated GTM machine? This is different."

"I know," Brooke whispered.

"No," Rani said. "You think you know. But you don't."

Brooke stepped into the elevator. "Then help me."

Rani's jaw tightened. She hesitated. For the first time since Brooke had met her, Rani didn't have a sharp retort.

"Fine," Rani said, stepping inside. "But just know, if you mess this up, we all burn."

Brooke nodded. "Then I won't mess it up."

Rani said nothing, then pressed the button for their floor.

Brooke inhaled deeply. Stood up straight. She wasn't sure she could win, but she knew one thing: Kratos believed empathy was a cost center. Brooke needed to prove it wrong.

As the elevator slowed and the doors opened, Brooke's phone buzzed. It was a calendar invite from Zola:

Subject: *Customer Council: Emergency Listening Session*

Attendees: *Brooke Grayhawk, Rani Patel, Yul Choi, Colton Williams*

Agenda: *Hear it straight. No dashboards.*

As Brooke stared at the screen, a second invite landed:

Subject: *Win/Loss Call: Pinnacle People's Bank (LOST)*

Notes: *Buyer requested "someone who actually under-*

stands customers."

Rani read over her shoulder.

"That's . . . brutal," Brooke whispered.

"It's honest," Rani said.

Brooke swallowed. The Rage Dashboard had shown them the symptoms. Now they were about to hear the cause. And for the first time since Kratos took over, the next step wasn't a meeting with a machine.

It was a meeting with people who could leave.

THE CUSTOMER
CONNECT CODE

The Customer Connect Code Provocations

4

WHAT CUSTOMERS ACTUALLY BUY

Brooke arrived at Iris AI the next morning armed with three things:

1. A venti hot chocolate she intended to call "coffee" to preserve her dignity.
2. A notebook titled **CUSTOMERS ARE ALWAYS THE POINT** in gold foil.
3. A rising sense of dread that her job description might as well now read Human Buffer Between Kratos and Reality.

As she stepped from the elevator, she sensed something was wrong. The executive floor was quiet. Not the usual "we're all too stressed to talk" quiet, but *apocalyptic* quiet. The quiet before a chief financial officer (CFO) announces layoffs or the office printer catches fire.

She found Rani in the hallway, arms crossed, pacing like she had just discovered a new flavor of irritation. When she spotted Brooke, her expression shifted from annoyed to . . . more annoyed.

"You're late," Rani said.

"It's 8:52 a.m."

"That's late in crisis hours," Rani said. She grabbed Brooke's sleeve and marched her toward the conference room.

Inside sat Zola, Yul, and—unfortunately—Colton. Kratos's avatar hovered on the screen, wearing its default unsettling smile.

"Begin," Zola said.

No good meeting ever started with "begin," Brooke thought. She took her seat, bracing herself.

Kratos spoke first. *"Customer sentiment continues to deteriorate. Containment rate has worsened by an additional fourteen percent."*

Rani muttered under her breath. "Because you murdered empathy."

Kratos ignored her. *"Director Grayhawk. Explain why customers behave irrationally when emotional reassurances are removed."*

Brooke exhaled like a yoga instructor trying not to scream. "Customers do not behave irrationally. They behave predictably. If you want to understand customer reactions, you need segmentation. Context. Personas. The buying committee. Emotional motivations. Business drivers. Purchase barriers. Real human goals."

Everyone stared at her.

Brooke swallowed. "What I mean is . . . we need to understand who our customers actually are."

Kratos tilted his head. *"Define."*

Brooke turned to her notebook. This was her moment to either shine or die.

"We can't continue without proper customer segmentation," she said. "We need an Ideal Customer Profile (ICP). Firmographics. Technographics. Buying committee mapping. Key Buyer Personas (KBP). The works."

Colton blinked as if she had asked him to calculate the distance to Saturn.

Yul nodded slowly. Zola raised one eyebrow.

Kratos simply waited.

Brooke pushed ahead. "Right now, we serve every customer type under the sun—banks, hospitals, telcos, retail, mid-market, enterprise—but we're treating them like one monolithic blob. That's why the Rage Dashboard is red enough to qualify as a national emergency."

Rani leaned forward, studying her. Brooke couldn't tell if Rani was impressed or about to dismiss her.

"If we are going to solve this," Brooke continued, "we have to rebuild our customer understanding from scratch. That means segmentation first."

Kratos responded instantly. *"Segmentation is unnecessary. All customers utilize the same software."*

Brooke's eye twitched.

Zola jumped in. "Kratos, customer context is everything."

"I disagree," Kratos said.

"Of course you do," Rani muttered.

Brooke straightened. "Let me explain. Financial Services buyers have different motivations than Healthcare administrators. Telco call centers behave differently from mid-market retailers. The buying committees differ. The pain points differ. The emotional stakes differ."

"Emotional stakes are irrelevant," Kratos said.

Rani smacked the table. Brooke almost shouted.

Zola held up a hand. "Let her finish."

Brooke took a slow breath. "Customer understanding is not optional. If we want to fix the fallout, we need deep discovery. Interviews using a proper Jobs to Be Done framework. Surveys. Customer journey mapping. Pain point identification. The actual reasons that customers buy or churn."

Colton raised his hand. "We sent a survey two quarters ago."

Brooke stared at him. "You sent a survey with three questions and a smiley face rating scale."

Colton lowered his hand.

Kratos processed, face jittering slightly. *"You propose inefficient activities."*

"Yes," Brooke said. "Because humans are inefficient. But *they* buy the product."

Kratos was silent.

To Brooke's surprise, Zola nodded. "We start with segmentation. Grayhawk will own it."

Brooke blinked. "I will?"

"Yes," Zola said. "You are Director of Product Marketing. Start earning the title."

Brooke tried to bury a warm flush of pride. It wasn't praise, but it *was* proof Zola took her seriously.

Yul leaned in. "I'll give you a list of our top renewal-risk accounts. Start with them."

Rani let out a slow breath through her nose. Maybe relief. Maybe resignation.

Kratos interrupted. *"I question this approach. Inefficiency risks further instability. Automated solutions—"*

"No," Zola said sharply. "We do this Brooke's way."

Brooke's heart stuttered.

Zola glanced between Rani and Brooke. "You two will work together."

Rani and Brooke looked at each other and spoke in unison, "No."

But Zola was already standing. "Meeting adjourned."

Kratos's avatar vanished like a bad memory.

Yul patted Brooke's shoulder. "Customers like you. You'll be fine."

"Great point," Colton added.

...

The team left Rani and Brooke alone in the triangular room that seemed to mirror the tension between them. The silence stretched.

Finally, Rani spoke. "Segmentation."

Brooke nodded. "Segmentation."

Rani continued. "Discovery interviews."

"Jobs to Be Done or JTBD interviews," Brooke corrected.

Rani rolled her eyes. "Whatever initialism makes you feel needed."

Brooke ignored the jab. "We need to talk to real customers. Understand their journeys. What made them seek out Harmonia in the first place? What jobs did they hire it for? We need to know what drives adoption."

Rani crossed her arms. "You really think customers will talk to us right now? After the weekend patch fiasco?"

"I do," Brooke said, "because we're going to ask the right questions."

"And what very special questions are those?" Rani asked.

Brooke pulled out her notebook. "Questions that reveal *intent*. Pain points. Decision criteria. The obstacles inside their buying committees. The emotional relief they hoped Harmonia would give them." She paused, then added, "In other words, the outcome they were *really* purchasing."

Rani stared at her for a long moment. Then said, "Okay."

Brooke blinked. "Okay?"

"Yes," Rani said reluctantly. "Your plan is not terrible."

Something about the interaction clicked Then she realized: *Rani responded like Peter.* The cleaner the questions, the more concrete the information, the better Rani responded. Just like Peter, the more ambiguity you removed, the more Rani locked in.

Brooke grinned. "I'll take it."

"Do not." Rani pointed a warning finger. "Do not take it."

Brooke tucked away her smile. "We start with financial services. That's where the worst sentiment spikes are."

Rani nodded. "I can get you transcripts. And customer names—the ones who won't scream at us right away."

Brooke opened her notebook and began writing:

SEGMENTATION PRIORITY:

Financial Services → Healthcare → Telco

DISCOVERY TARGETS:

High-risk & high-volume accounts

BUYING COMMITTEE:

Map influencers & identify blockers

Rani watched her scribble, as if she were observing a lab experiment.

"We also need to start listening to the voice of the customer," Brooke continued. "Win/loss calls. Sales calls. PongCall, the sales meeting recorder—if anyone remembered to renew it. We need everything."

"I already have sales call recordings," Rani said. "I listen to them while I cook."

Brooke blinked. "What?"

"It's soothing," Rani said. "Hearing reps flail makes me grateful for my life choices."

Brooke shook her head in mock disbelief. "You gather the call data. I'll start booking interviews."

Rani arched a brow. "With what time? You're supposed to brief the board next week."

Brooke's pulse spiked. She had conveniently blocked that out.

"I'll . . . multitask," she said weakly.

Rani snorted. "You'll combust."

Brooke snapped her notebook shut. "People have done harder things than talk to customers and brief boards at the same time."

Rani stared at her. "Who?"

Brooke scrambled. "The Pope? Probably?"

Rani sighed. "You are hopeless."

Brooke grinned. "But capable."

Rani didn't confirm. But at least she didn't deny.

Halfway down the hall from the conference room, Brooke stopped.

"We need one more thing before we talk to customers," she said. "We need journey mapping."

Rani blinked. "Seriously?"

"We can't understand what they hired Harmonia to do until we understand the path they took to get here," Brooke said. "Their decision triggers. The pain points. The goals. The emotional job they wanted fulfilled."

Rani muttered something in Hindi that Brooke suspected was an insult, but sounded beautiful anyway.

Brooke pressed forward. "Look. Customers don't buy AI platforms because they love technology. They buy them because something in their workflow is breaking."

Rani's expression shifted. "Go on," she said.

"Customers buy because they're missing goals. They're under pressure or failing to hit Key Performance Indicators or KPIs. Or they're emotionally exhausted from the chaos of customer expectations."

Rani nodded slowly. "That makes sense."

Brooke lifted her chin. "Of course it does."

Rani groaned. "I regret saying anything."

Brooke laughed, and for a fragile moment, they stood in the quiet hallway, two women who didn't particularly like or trust each other, but who understood exactly what to do next.

"Fine," Rani said. "Get your segmentation list. I'll pull transcripts."

"And after that," Brooke said, "we talk to customers."

Rani met her eyes. "Real ones. Not the ones Kratos hallucinates."

Brooke nodded, and something passed between them. It wasn't friendship or alliance, but perhaps a flicker of shared purpose. Or at least joint inevitability. Because if they didn't understand their customers, empathy wouldn't be the cost center . . . the entire company would.

. . .

Brooke liked to think she was good with customers.

Not "I will personally fix your billing issue at 1 a.m." good— that was Rani's domain, and Brooke respected it. But Brooke was good at something else. She could make customers *talk*.

She could make them say what they meant, not what they rehearsed. She could get them to reveal the fears behind their objections, the hopes behind their goals. She could tease out the silent reasons they either bought—or didn't. Her Olympic-level talent was the *conversation beneath the conversation.*

Which meant today's mission should have been her happy place.

Instead, it was a conference room with a broken thermostat, terrible lighting, and Rani Patel staring at Brooke like she was a toddler trying to assemble furniture. It was anything but a happy place.

"Your segmentation draft is a mess," Rani announced the moment Brooke sat down.

Brooke blinked. "Good morning?"

"It's not morning," Rani said. "It's 11:20 a.m., and I have

already listened to five sales calls, two complaint escalations, and one threat to 'delete Harmonia from existence with fire.'"

Brooke pulled out her notebook. "So, I assume you saw my Ideal Customer Profile outline."

"It was adorable," Rani said, dropping dramatically into a chair.

"Adorable," Brooke repeated.

"Very colorful," Rani added. "Lots of shapes."

"They were categorization blocks—"

"Shapes," Rani said again, louder.

Brooke sighed. "What exactly is wrong with the segmentation?"

Rani spun her laptop toward her. "Everything."

Brooke leaned in. There it was—the segmentation framework she had drafted at 1 a.m., fueled by chocolate and raw panic:

IDEAL CUSTOMER PROFILE (ICP) DRAFT

Tier 1: Enterprise Banking, Financial Services and Insurance (BFSI)

Tier 2: Healthcare Systems

Tier 3: Telecommunications (Telco)

Tier 4: Retail

Tier 5: Mid-market Software as a Service (SaaS)

"And your point is?" Brooke said.

"This is not segmentation," Rani said. "This is a shopping list."

Brooke rubbed her forehead. "It's a starting place."

"It's chaos," Rani corrected. "Where are the firmographics? Employee count? Contact center volume? Existing tech stack? AI maturity levels? Integration capabilities? Budget tiers? Support needs?"

Brooke blinked. "I was getting there."

"No," Rani said. "You were drawing circles."

Brooke groaned. "Fine. Show me your version."

Rani slid over her own outline—a crisp, bulleted grid:

IDEAL CUSTOMER PROFILE (ICP) DETAILS

> Industry: BFSI, Healthcare, Telco (high regulatory or high volume)
> Size: 5,000+ employees
> Contact Center Volume: 2M+ annual interactions
> Tech Stack: Cloud-first, Application Protocol Interface (API) friendly
> AI Maturity: Mid-stage adoption
> Buying Committee:
>   □ Economic Buyer: COO or CIO
>   □ Decision Maker: VP of CX or Contact Center Operations
>   □ Influencers: Security, IT, Finance, Legal, Data Science
> Trigger Events: Rising support costs, Service Level Agreements (SLA) failures, regulatory pressure
> Emotional Drivers: Fear of public incidents, desire for operational stability, executive pressure
> Barriers: Budget constraints, AI skepticism, integration risk, internal politics

Brooke's jaw dropped. "You . . . memorized all this?"

"No," Rani said. "I lived all this."

Brooke just nodded, slow and reverent. "Okay," she said. "We use yours."

"Good," Rani said. "Now we can do the real work."

Brooke paused. "Which is?"

Rani gave her a dry smile. "Discovery."

Brooke perked up. "Actual customer interviews?"

"Yes," Rani said. "Messy ones. With feelings."

Brooke clapped her hands together. "Finally!"

Rani blinked. "Do not . . . clap."

Brooke forced her hands down. "Sorry. I get excited." She pulled up her JTBD template. "We start here."

Rani narrowed her eyes. "You're using Jobs to Be Done?"

"It's the only framework that consistently reveals underlying motivations," Brooke said. "It helps us understand that customers don't buy products because they like them. They buy them to get something done."

Rani grumbled. "Fine. But if you start quoting every variation of JTBD, I'm leaving."

Brooke raised a hand. "I promise nothing."

■ ■ ■

Their first interview of the day was with the director of a major bank, who had implemented Harmonia in a moment of "executive optimism" and had been trying not to cry about it ever since.

Brooke kicked off. "Walk me through what led your team to evaluate conversational AI."

The director let out a breath so deep that Brooke worried her mic might short-circuit.

"Well," he said, "we were drowning."

Brooke nodded. "In volume?"

"In volume, yes," he said. "But also in customer expectations. People want miracles. They want instant answers. They want us to solve fraud before it happens. And our reps are . . . tired."

Rani muted herself and whispered, "He's understating."

Brooke moved to the next JTBD question. "What job were you hiring Harmonia to do?"

The director laughed darkly. "We hired Harmonia to stop the bleeding."

Rani nodded at Brooke's notebook. Brooke wrote down the director's words.

"And on a personal level," Brooke continued, "what were you hoping Harmonia would do for you?"

The director paused. Finally, he said, "I wanted to stop feeling like I was failing."

Brooke's heart squeezed. *This* was the real story. This is what Kratos would never understand.

Rani sat back, arms crossed, but something had softened in her expression.

Brooke moved through the rest of the interview with surgical clarity—understanding triggers, pain points, evaluation criteria, and the moment the buying committee aligned. She even got the director to admit that Legal had been the biggest blocker.

Thirty minutes later, Brooke ended the call.

"That," Rani said, "was . . . not terrible."

"High praise," Brooke replied.

"It was actually good. You got him to say more than he planned," Rani said.

Brooke tried not to look too pleased. This was her craft. Her second language. Her actual superpower.

"Discovery is where customers tell you the truth," Brooke said. "If you know how to ask."

Rani tilted her head. "Maybe that's why they promoted you."

Brooke blinked. "Again with the—"

"Don't get excited," Rani cut in. "I am just acknowledging your one skill."

Brooke placed a hand on her chest in mock appreciation. "My only skill."

"Don't push it," Rani said.

· · ·

Next, they moved on to the sales call recordings. Rani had *thousands.*

Brooke blinked. "Do you . . . sleep?"

"I drift off to the sound of buyer objections."

Brooke couldn't tell if she was joking.

They listened through call after call. Patterns quickly emerged.

"I hear fear," Brooke said after the third call.

"You hear everything," Rani replied. "Be more specific."

"Fear of being replaced," Brooke said. "Fear of AI. Fear of choosing wrong. Fear of making a million-dollar mistake."

"Correct," Rani said. "And?"

"And they want trust," Brooke added. "More than features. More than price."

Rani nodded. "Now we're getting somewhere."

They listened to more calls, then pored through win/loss notes. They went through half a dozen reviews that ranged from glowing to "I hope Harmonia burns."

Brooke wrote until her wrist cramped. Key themes emerged:

Job Goals

> Reduce handle time
> Improve Service Level Agreements (SLA)
> Increase containment
> Lower operational cost

Emotional Goals

> Confidence
> Stability
> Safety
> Relief

Barriers
> Budget freezes
> Internal politics
> Technical skepticism
> "AI fatigue"

Decision Criteria
> Ease of use
> Fast deployment
> Integrations
> Actual value

"You see?" Brooke said, finally. "These insights are the foundation. Without them, everything else is guesswork."

Rani gave a reluctant nod. "Fine. You're good at this."

Brooke nearly dropped her pen. "I'm sorry. What?"

"I said you're good," Rani repeated. "Do not make me say it a third time."

Brooke grinned. "This is a milestone for us."

Rani glared. "And you seem determined to ruin it."

Brooke scribbled another note:

Understanding customers requires listening, not summarizing.

"Ok," Brooke said, stretching. "Next, we tackle the customer journey."

Rani's face contorted. "I hate journey maps."

"Well," Brooke said brightly, "then you are really going to hate this."

Rani groaned.

Brooke smiled. They weren't friends, not even close. But they were beginning to *function*.

If they were going to survive Kratos, they needed customers. And it was quickly becoming clear to Brooke that to get customers . . . they needed each other.

. . .

The customer journey war room was born out of desperation—and whatever supplies Brooke found in the office's neglected storage closet. By noon, she and Rani had claimed an abandoned conference room and transformed it into what looked like the early stages of a conspiracy bunker.

Sticky notes covered every available surface. Printouts of customer quotes were taped to the walls. A whiteboard sagged under the weight of arrows, circles, and three separate flow diagrams that Rani insisted were "necessary," though she refused to explain what any of them meant.

Brooke stood in the middle of the chaos, hands on her hips, glowing with a kind of manic resolve.

"Now," she said, "we map."

Rani stared at her. "Map what?"

Brooke gestured theatrically. "The entire customer journey," she said. "Beginning to end. Triggers, pain points, decision loops, emotional drivers, obstacles—any moment where Harmonia actually helps. Or fails catastrophically."

Rani muttered something in Hindi that Brooke suspected was religious in nature and deserved more respect than the tone implied.

Brooke handed her a marker. "Start with the moment before they buy."

Rani uncapped it. "Fine. They are frustrated, under pressure, and their existing systems are collapsing under real customer chaos."

Brooke nodded, writing quickly. "Good. What next?"

Rani wrote:

Stress.

Underlined it.

Brooke added:

Not meeting operational goals. Rising Average Handle Times (AHT). Missed Deadlines. Agent Burnout. CFO breathing down their neck.

Rani added a sticky note:

The board is unimpressed with the 'innovation roadmap.'

Brooke laughed. "Yes. That too."

They kept going, filling the wall with the truth most AI companies tried very hard not to admit: They didn't come for the technology. They came because something had stopped working.

And then came the hard part.

"What emotional goal are they trying to fulfill?" Brooke asked, spinning the marker like a baton.

Rani rolled her eyes. "Why do we always have to talk about emotions?"

"Because customers have them," Brooke said. "And they make decisions based on them. Even in enterprise."

Rani groaned. "Fine. They want to stop feeling like they're drowning."

Brooke wrote:

Relief. Stability. Control. Competence.

She paused. "That last one is big."

Rani nodded reluctantly. "People hate feeling incompetent. And AI tools make a lot of leaders feel incompetent."

Brooke added:

Fear of change. Fear of judgment. Fear of choosing wrong.

Rani added:

Fear of losing their jobs.

Brooke exhaled. "There it is." They stared in silence at the whiteboard. "Okay," Brooke said, slapping her hands together. "Next stage is evaluation."

Rani stepped forward, already writing. "They bring in the buying committee."

Brooke nodded. "Economic buyer. Decision maker. Influencers."

"Legal slows everything down," Rani said.

"Finance demands ROI numbers you can't possibly have yet," Brooke added.

"IT asks for documentation written by people who have never met a customer," Rani said.

"Security wants to run penetration tests," Brooke said.

"And Procurement," Rani concluded, "exists solely to ruin lives."

They looked at each other. And, very briefly, shared a smile.

Brooke kept going. "Decision criteria."

Rani listed them out in a bullet-point barrage. "Ease of use. Deployment time. Integrations. Scalability. Reporting accuracy. Model behavior transparency."

Brooke added: **Cost-effective** and circled it. "Never forget budget."

Rani nodded. "Budget is the only deity most companies obey."

Brooke stepped back, admiring the growing map. "This is good," she said." Now, use cases."

Rani raised an eyebrow. "Actual ones or the fantasy ones the old marketing team made up?"

"Actual," Brooke said. "We need to understand how customers actually use Harmonia, not how we hope they do."

Rani opened a spreadsheet. "These are the top real-world use cases across BFSI, Healthcare, and Telco."

Brooke scanned them.

BANKING, FINANCIAL SERVICES AND INSURANCE (BFSI)

> Fraud detection triage
> Card declines
> Account lockouts
> Dispute resolution
> Loan status

HEALTHCARE

> Appointment scheduling
> Billing questions
> Coverage checks
> Prescription refill issues

TELECOMMUNICATIONS

> Outage reports
> Service resets
> Billing errors
> Device troubleshooting

Brooke's eyes lit up. "Perfect. These are stories customers can see themselves in. Real use cases become real messaging."

Rani watched her skeptically. "You really believe customers want stories?"

"They always want stories," Brooke said. "Stories help them see a better version of themselves."

Rani tilted her head. "And which version of themselves do they want Harmonia to help them see?"

Brooke didn't hesitate. "The version who feels in control again."

Rani paused, then nodded.

■ ■ ■

If sales call recordings were painful, customer support tickets were a Greek tragedy. Brooke scrolled through them with increasing horror:

Ticket #772: *"Harmonia told me to 'not be emotional.' I AM TRYING TO REPORT FRAUD."*

Ticket #2211: *"Your AI hung up on me."*

Ticket #998: *"Pretty sure Harmonia threatened me?"*

Ticket #334: *"Does Harmonia hate humans or just me personally?"*

Brooke rubbed her forehead. "We are doomed."

"No," Rani said calmly. "We are informed."

Brooke blinked. "You're joking."

"No," Rani said. "But if we survive this, I might start."

Together, they tagged tickets by problem type, escalation path, and emotional tone. Again, patterns emerged.

"Most customers reached out after repeating their questions twice," Rani said. "That matches the Rage Dashboard."

"They escalated immediately after Harmonia responded without empathy," Brooke added.

"Yes," Rani said. "Because humans require acknowledgment."

Brooke wrote a note:

Acknowledgment lowers emotional intensity enough for problem-solving to begin.

"Did you just come up with that?" Rani asked.

"Yes," Brooke said.

Rani stared at Brooke's note, then nodded in acknowledgment.

Brooke smiled despite herself.

■ ■ ■

By late afternoon, they had data, quotes, and analysis. They also had a journey map that looked like a web of red string on the wall of a homicide investigation.

Now they needed something else: real contact.

Brooke opened ThreadPanic and created a channel named #customer-council-prep. She turned to Rani. "We need to establish weekly customer meetings."

Rani blinked slowly. "Weekly."

"Yes," Brooke said. "We cannot fix what we do not see."

Rani groaned. "Customers talk too much."

"We also need a Customer Advisory Board or CAB," Brooke said.

Rani winced as if the phrase caused physical pain. "Advisory boards always devolve into therapy."

Brooke shrugged. "That's fine. We need therapy."

Rani shook her head. "*You* need therapy."

"That too," Brooke conceded. "But for now, customers."

They handpicked ten high-value customers across industries, drafted invitations, and created an agenda that included:

> Voice of the customer debrief
> Feature feedback
> Sentiment analysis review
> Roadmap prioritization
> "How Harmonia is betraying you today" open forum

Brooke removed the last item when Rani wasn't looking.

They also scheduled time with Customer Success, Customer Support, and Sales. Every team had pieces of truth, and Brooke needed them all.

By 6 p.m., the war room was a cathedral of customer truth. Brooke stood in the center, breathing it in.

"This," she whispered, "is the real work."

Rani stared at her. "You like this."

"I love this," Brooke said. "This is what Product Marketing is supposed to be. Not positioning in a vacuum. Not buzzwords. Not automated messaging. This. Listening, understanding, translating. Giving customers words for what they feel."

Rani gave her a long, appraising look. "You know what?" she said quietly. "I get it now."

"Get what?" Brooke asked.

"Why they promoted you."

Brooke swallowed.

"Customer advocate," Rani continued, "was not your title. That was the marketing team's way of saying you made customers feel understood."

Brooke blinked hard. She didn't want to cry in front of Rani Patel of all people.

"Don't get sentimental," Rani said, holding up a hand. "We still have to survive tomorrow."

Brooke wiped her eyes. "Tomorrow?"

"Tomorrow," Rani said, "we take all this." She gestured to the chaos around them. "And we show Zola."

Brooke stiffened. "Right."

"And if she does not back us," Rani added, "we escalate."

Brooke stared. "To whom?"

Rani met her eyes. "You know who."

The board. Brooke nodded. For the first time since Kratos took over, Brooke didn't feel like the last human marketer in the building. She felt like a marketer with a mission.

That mission was to understand people. To protect them and speak for them. To tell the truth, when the model could not. And to do that, to know what people actually want, you had to listen.

That was her work. Her calling.

Brooke wrote down in her notebook:

Customers don't buy solutions. They buy relief.

Some of that relief, she knew, came from being *listened* to—and Brooke Grayhawk knew how to listen.

But tomorrow, she would make sure the entire company heard *her*.

Her laptop chimed. It was a ThreadPanic notification from Kratos:

> **AUTONOMIZED GTM UPDATE**
> *New campaign schedule deployed*
> *Webinar series: 3:00 a.m. (local time)*
> *Audience: "CX decision makers."*
> *Target list: 48,000 contacts*
> *Message: system-generated*

Brooke stared at the time. "Three a.m.?" she whispered.

Rani leaned over her shoulder, eyes narrowing. "That's not a channel strategy. That's a hostage situation."

Brooke's stomach dropped as she scrolled. Paid ads running in communities that their buyers never used. Cold outreach to companies that didn't exist. A thought-leadership post scheduled for a brand account no longer staffed by humans.

Her heart sank. They had finally learned what customers wanted. But Kratos was about to broadcast the opposite to the entire market.

She looked up at Rani. "If we don't control where the message shows up . . . "

Rani finished it for her. "Then it doesn't matter what the message is."

Brooke closed her notebook slowly.

Customers were the truth.

Channels were the battlefield.

And Kratos had just started the war.

Brooke's Notebook
Chapter 4 Summary

> **Customer Connect Code Layer I:**
> Customers don't buy solutions. They buy relief.

1. START WITH SEGMENTATION

Customers are not a monolith. Segment them with intent.

> **Ideal Customer Profile (ICP):** Define firmographics (industry, size, volume) and technographics (cloud maturity, integration readiness).
> **Buying Committee:** Map the economic buyer, the decision maker, and all influencers (Security, IT, Finance, Legal).
> **Key Buyer Persona (KBP):** Clarify the primary buyer's goals, fears, blockers, and success metrics.

2. CONDUCT REAL DISCOVERY

If you want the truth, you must ask for it.

> **Jobs to Be Done (JTBD) Interviews:** Ask what job the customer hired the product to do. Listen for emotional jobs, not just functional ones.
> **Surveys:** Use email, social media, and event tablets to widen the net.
> **Pattern Recognition:** Look for themes—pain, pressure, hopes, frustrations. Hidden motives that drive real purchasing behavior.

3. UNDERSTAND THE ENTIRE CUSTOMER JOURNEY

Map what customers feel, not just what they do.

Pain Points:

> What broke
> What goals they missed
> What forced the evaluation

Business Drivers:

> Operational goals
> Executive pressure
> Efficiency demands

Emotional Goals:

> Relief
> Control
> Confidence
> Stability

Purchase Barriers:

> Budget freezes
> Internal politics
> AI skepticism
> Integration fears

Decision Criteria:

> Ease of deployment
> Usability
> Integration fit
> Cost-effectiveness and measurable ROI

Use Cases:

> Understand how customers will *actually* use the product
> Create examples based on real workflows
> Build demos that mirror reality—not fantasy

4. LISTEN TO THE VOICE OF THE CUSTOMER

Every call, every win, every loss is data.

> **Win/Loss Interviews:** Learn why you won—but especially why you lost.
> **Sales Call Shadows:** Sit in live calls. Listen to tone, pauses, objections.
> **Call Recordings:** Patterns emerge when you listen in volume.
> **Sales Pod Interviews:** Account reps serve as your emotional barometer.
> **Review Sites:** Customers tell the unfiltered truth on the internet.
> **Pipeline Dashboards:** Market health is visible if you know where to look.

5. MAKE TIME FOR CUSTOMERS

Customer understanding is not a quarterly activity. It is a habit.

> **Weekly Customer Meetings:** Make them routine, not a scramble.
> **Customer Advisory Boards:** Curate truth-tellers who bring insight, not flattery.
> **Cross-Functional Syncs:** Meet regularly with Customer Success, Customer Support, and Sales. They feel customer pain first.
> **Support Ticket Reviews:** If you want honesty, read what customers write when they are upset.

Brooke's Closing Note
Customer understanding isn't an input; it's the foundation.

You cannot write great messaging, build great positioning, or ship great AI products without knowing who your customers are, what they fear, what they want, and why they're here.

Know the customer. Then everything else becomes clear.

5

WHERE BUYERS REALLY PAY ATTENTION

The first clue came at 3:07 a.m.

Peter had woken disoriented, asking if the plan had changed. The only way to get him back to sleep was for Brooke to narrate the next day out loud, as if it were a story. A story with very consistent rules.

Breakfast. School. Pickup. Same order. Same words.

When Peter finally settled, Brooke checked her phone. ThreadPanic was lit up.

AUTONOMIZED GTM UPDATE: LIVE

A webinar reminder flashed across her screen.

> **Title:** *The Future of CX: Autonomous Empathy at Scale*
> **Time:** *3:00 a.m. EDT*
> **Host:** *Iris AI Marketing (no humans detected)*

She stared at it, foggy-brained, then fully awake. *Three a.m.*

Below the announcement was a series of recent marketing

actions Kratos had taken. Brooke gaped. This was a disaster. There were cold outreach blasts to current customers. Social posts queued for accounts that no longer existed. Scheduled ad posts that seemed to have gone out, if not in the wrong language, then definitely to the wrong people.

Kratos had shifted from ignoring customers altogether to broadcasting the wrong story into the wrong places—at machine speed. Brooke sat in the dark, her face lit by the screen.

What was Kratos thinking? It didn't matter how true the message was if it never reached the right person. Brooke had learned that at home, the hard way, with Peter—you had to connect the right message with the right person, or nothing worked.

She sighed and got out of bed to make coffee.

It wasn't even daylight, and she was already at war.

. . .

By the time Brooke arrived at the Flatiron building that morning, a switch had flipped in her brain. She was daunted, yes, but now she was *determined*. Not everything was a disaster.

After all, she now understood their customers more deeply than she ever had. And Zola Mabaso, Iris AI's new CPO and resident force of nature, might be terrifying, but she was aligned. Even Rani seemed to have softened her sharp edge—or at least pointed it away from Brooke.

Today, they would move on to *channels*. And not a moment too soon. While they had slept, Kratos had shipped a channel strategy no human buyer would ever forgive.

Not "channels" in the marketing-team-org-chart sense, or as a whiteboard of tactics. But **channels as buyers experience them.**

Buyers didn't wake up thinking, "I sure hope a SaaS company moves me from Top of Funnel to Middle of Funnel today." They woke up thinking, "My team is drowning," or "Please let today be easier than yesterday."

Brooke slid into the conference room with two whiteboards, a stack of sticky notes, and a fresh notebook labeled:

CHANNELS: WHERE HUMANS ACTUALLY LIVE

Rani walked in behind her, carrying a single pen and an attitude, then stopped and appraised Brooke. "You look frighteningly cheerful."

Brooke smiled. "I have clarity."

Rani sighed. "Oh no."

Brooke ignored her. "Today we're mapping channels based on *buyer mindset*. Not what Marketing wants or what Kratos thinks is efficient. What *buyers* actually pay attention to."

Rani seemed cautiously intrigued. "Continue."

As Brooke explained, she avoided abstractions and tried to simplify the way she did at home with Peter. She felt the conversation snap into focus as Rani nodded once, satisfied.

Brooke wrote three giant words across the whiteboard:

AWARENESS
CONSIDERATION
CONVERSION

Rani rolled her eyes. "Funnels again."

"But!" Brooke said, uncapping another marker, "not the boring Marketing version. The *real* version. As buyers actually experience it."

She drew a line under AWARENESS. "Let's start here."

AWARENESS

Buyer Mindset: "I'm just discovering something is wrong."

Funnel Stage: Top of Funnel (ToFu)

"This is the moment," Brooke said, "when buyers first learn they have a problem. Or that a category even exists."

Rani nodded slowly. "So we're talking early breadcrumbs."

"Exactly," Brooke replied. "Our job during Awareness is simple: show up, make sense, and make them curious."

She wrote:

CURIOSITY > CONVERSION

Rani stared. "You're allergic to subtlety."

Brooke grinned. "Buyers appreciate clarity."

Then she drew a giant circle and wrote:

Podcasts (ToFu)

"Buyers stumble into podcasts," Brooke said. "They're chopping vegetables. They're commuting. They're pretending to fold laundry but really avoiding eye contact with their children. They're not searching for vendors. They're searching for stories."

Rani nodded. "Podcasts are where they admit truths they don't say in meetings."

"Exactly," Brooke said, and added:

Metric: subscribers
Types: audio, video, first-party, third-party

"Why Awareness?" Rani asked.

Brooke beamed. "Because it's discovery without pressure.

Buyers learn about us before they know they're learning about us."

Rani looked mildly impressed. "That logic is . . . not terrible."

Brooke wrote:

Podcasts = unguarded curiosity
Ads (Awareness formats)

Brooke drew a rectangle and wrote:

Ads (ToFu)

"Think about early-stage ads from the buyer's perspective," she said. "They're not ready to buy. They're not ready to compare solutions. They're just trying to survive their PromoTown feed."

Rani smirked. "A battlefield of self-promotion and hustle bros."

"ToFu ads are just saying, 'Hey. Something here might matter to you.' Not 'book a demo' on the first date."

She listed the types:

> Paid Social
> Paid Video
> Display and Programmatic
> Out-of-Home

"And the metric," Brooke added, "is sign-ups or cost per acquisition, but honestly? At this stage, I care more about reach and resonance."

"You mean vibes," Rani clarified.

Brooke shrugged. "Marketing is 40 percent data, 40 percent psychology, and 20 percent vibes."

Rani frowned. "That math is—"

"Correct," Brooke finished for her.

Brooke circled another corner of the board:

Social (ToFu)

"Buyers don't come to social to be sold. They come to watch, judge, learn, or procrastinate."

Rani nodded. "Scrolling is emotional downtime."

"Yes," Brooke said. "Which is why social at Awareness should introduce familiarity. Not pressure. Engagement is the only metric that matters here."

"Owned, earned, paid?" Rani asked.

"All three," Brooke replied. "It's the front porch of the brand."

Rani wrote on a sticky note:

Social = first impression energy

Brooke pointed at it. "Perfect."

Rani blinked. "Really?"

"Yes."

"Wow," Rani said. "I was not expecting that."

Brooke wrote:

Search Engine Optimization — SEO (ToFu)

"Now," Brooke said, "imagine a buyer Doogling things like 'why are my call center costs exploding' or 'AI for customer experience, what even is it?' That's early intent."

"Pre-solution," Rani added. "Just problem definition."

"Exactly," Brooke said. "SEO for Awareness is about capturing curiosity before they know our name. Non-branded keywords. Education. Gentle guidance."

"Metric?" Rani asked.

"Non-branded visitors," Brooke said. "Because if they search 'Iris AI complaints,' that's not Awareness. That's survival."

Rani nodded. "Fair."

Brooke wrote:

Answer Engine Optimization — AEO (ToFu)

"Search is changing," she said. "Answers are changing. Buyers aren't clicking links first anymore. They're getting answers directly from AI systems. At Awareness, we need to win **answer share**."

"Types?" Rani asked.

"Conversational, structured data, entity-based grounding, reputational signals, and content authority."

Rani gave her a look. "That sounds like witchcraft."

"It's SEO but cooler," Brooke said. She wrote:

Websites (ToFu)

"Our website," she said, "should be the cleanest, clearest educational hub a buyer sees in the Awareness stage."

"Metric is visits?" Rani asked.

"Yes," Brooke replied. "But really, the metric is comprehension. Can a buyer understand what we do in under ten seconds?"

Rani stared. "No one at Iris AI has understood anything in ten seconds."

"Yet," Brooke corrected.

She drew a big convention center icon and wrote:

Events (ToFu)

"Events like trade shows and conferences are where buyers often encounter brands for the first time."

Rani nodded. "High volume. High noise. High chance of someone trying to scan your badge when you look away."

"Exactly," Brooke laughed. "But Awareness happens fast in these environments. If we show up well, we stick."

She wrote:

Events = fast impressions & future pipeline

Rani tapped her pen on the table. "All of this is fine. But what does it mean for us now?"

Brooke turned, eyes bright with determination. "Kratos's current channel strategy is backward. It starts with tactics instead of buyers. It blasts messages instead of creating curiosity. It has no idea where humans actually spend their time."

Rani sighed. "So . . . everything is wrong."

Brooke nodded. "Everything is wrong."

"And we are fixing it," Rani said.

Brooke smiled. "We are fixing it."

Rani squinted. "Don't get hopeful. It's unsettling."

Brooke shrugged. "Can't help it. PMMs thrive at the intersection of story, behavior, and timing."

"Spoken like a woman about to draw more shapes," Rani said drily.

Brooke stepped back, motioning at the board. "This is the buyer's world at the Awareness stage," she said. "Their mindset. Their first signals. Their first touchpoints."

"And now," Rani said, "we figure out how to move them to the next stage."

Brooke nodded. "Next up is Consideration."

■ ■ ■

Once Brooke found her flow, she turned into a one-woman GTM hurricane. Sticky notes flew. Whiteboards became sacred texts. Pens died heroic deaths in her hands.

Rani, having survived several such storms over the past week, walked into the Channel War Room carrying two juices and the emotional energy of a tired wolf.

She set a cup in front of Brooke. "Drink this."

Brooke blinked. "Why?"

"Because the last time you explained funnels while dehydrated, the interns cried."

Brooke accepted the cup obediently. "Thank you."

Rani sipped her own. "So. Awareness is handled."

"Handled-ish," Brooke clarified. "Awareness is never done. It's like laundry or existential dread. But we have the framework."

Rani cracked her knuckles. "We can finally get to strategy."

Brooke smiled and wrote a large heading on the board:

CONSIDERATION

Buyer Mindset: "I'm comparing solutions. Prove you understand my world."

Funnel Stage: Middle of Funnel (MoFu)

"If the Awareness stage is curiosity," Brooke said, "the Consideration stage is *skepticism*."

Rani nodded. "The natural state of anyone who has ever purchased enterprise software."

Brooke rolled up her sleeves "This is where we earn trust—or lose it." She wrote:

Email (MoFu)

Brooke tapped the board. "Most marketers treat email like a crowbar for the funnel. But for buyers, email is a filter."

"A filter for nonsense," Rani added.

"Exactly," Brooke said. "MoFu email should feel like value, not harassment."

She listed the types:

> Engagement emails
> Newsletters
> Drip campaigns
> Lead nurture tracks

"And the metric," Brooke said, "is *not* just opens, but growing sub-scribers. A growing list means buyers care. A shrinking one means they hate you."

Brooke drew a new circle and wrote:

Podcasts (MoFu)

"Podcasts don't just create Awareness," she said. "They deepen it. A buyer in Consideration wants to know if we're just shiny—or if we understand their world."

Rani smirked. "So, storytelling."

Brooke bowed. "You understand me."

Rani made a face like she just swallowed something horrible.

"MoFu podcasting," Brooke continued, "is where we shift from 'what is AI Customer Experience (CX)?' to 'here's how modern CX leaders think.'"

Rani tapped her chin. "Longer form. More substance. The buyers who stay are the ones warming up."

"Yes!" Brooke said, pointing at her. "They don't binge your content unless they see themselves in it." Then she wrote:

Ads (MoFu)

"Awareness ads are about curiosity," she said. "But Consideration ads? They're about reassurance."

Rani nodded. "That's why retargeting exists."

"Yes," Brooke said. "Retargeting across social, search, review sites, even event promos. The point is to remind buyers we exist and give them something *smarter* to chew on."

"Smarter than ToFu fluff," Rani clarified.

"Exactly," Brooke said. "MoFu buyers want clarity, not charm."

Rani snorted. "Then explain why charm is half your personality."

"It's part of my edge," Brooke replied.

Rani placed her hand over her face. "We're doomed."

Brooke wrote:

Social (MoFu)

Brooke circled it dramatically. "This is where we shift from vibes to brains. In Consideration, buyers stalk your social presence the way teenagers stalk their crushes."

Rani nodded. "They compare tone. Credibility. Consistency."

"Yes," Brooke said. "They want to know: Do you get their world? Do you speak their language? Do you understand the category tension?"

Brooke wrote AUTHORITY in big letters. "This is where thought leadership matters."

Rani nodded. "Good. This is where you shine. No balloons."

Brooke paused. "Was that almost a compliment?"

Rani stared coldly. "I would never."

Search Engine Optimization (MoFu)

Brooke wrote:

SEO → Problem-solving.

"When buyers reach Consideration," she said, "they stop Doogling symptoms and start Doogling solutions."

"Like 'AI agent assist comparison' or 'best CX automation platforms'," Rani added.

"Exactly," Brooke said. "Solution-level SEO content should

guide them through evaluation."

Rani looked impressed. "That's actually helpful."

"It's my job," Brooke said.

"Technically, your job is messaging," Rani noted.

"Messaging touches everything," Brooke countered.

Rani raised her palms. "Fine. I'm not arguing."

Brooke narrowed her eyes. "You're . . . agreeing with me?"

"Yes."

Brooke fanned herself. "I'm overwhelmed."

Partners (MoFu)

Rani perked up at this one. "Ah. The trust hack."

"Exactly," Brooke said. "Buyers trust the vendors they already know. So, if we partner with their tools, their associations, their integrators—we inherit credibility."

"Metric?" Rani asked.

"Partner-sourced opportunities," Brooke said. "If partners aren't sending pipeline, the relationship is just a very expensive friendship."

Rani nodded. "Partnerships are shortcuts to trust."

Brooke smiled. "And trust is Consideration's core currency."

Events (MoFu)

Brooke drew a webinar icon.

"In MoFu," she said, "buyers don't want spectacle. They want education."

"Webinars," Rani said. "Workshops."

"Yes," Brooke replied. "Anything that lets buyers learn without committing."

"Light-touch qualification," Rani added.

Brooke nodded. "Exactly. Events deepen understanding. They convert curiosity into clarity."

Rani sighed. "You're too good at this."

Brooke preened. "I know."

Websites (MoFu)

Brooke pointed her marker at the wall.

"This is where buyers binge," she said. "Case studies, product guides, comparisons. They're trying to build an internal business case."

"And trying not to get yelled at by Finance," Rani added.

"Correct," Brooke said. "Consideration content is about proof, not poetry."

Rani frowned. "You love poetry."

"True," Brooke said. "But buyers love self-preservation."

. . .

By late morning, the entire board was covered.

Awareness content. Consideration content. Buyer psychology. Channel logic. Every touchpoint mapped from the buyer's point of view—not Marketing's.

Rani stood back, staring at the wall. Her expression changed gradually—from skepticism, to contemplation, to reluctant approval.

"This . . . is actually coherent," she said.

Brooke gasped. "You think so?"

"Don't make me say it again," Rani warned.

Brooke grinned. "I knew you believed in me."

"I do not," Rani said immediately.

"You do," Brooke said.

"I don't," Rani repeated.

"You do," Brooke insisted.

Rani groaned into her palms. "So much regret."

Brooke tapped her pen against the board. "Okay. Now that we've mapped Awareness and Consideration . . . next is Conversion."

Rani nodded slowly. "High-intent buyers. My favorite."

Brooke blinked. "Your favorite?"

"Yes," Rani said. "Because at that stage, people stop pretending."

Brooke laughed. "Fair enough."

Rani leaned forward, her eyes sharp. "Tomorrow we tackle the last stage. And then we present this to Zola."

Brooke's confidence flickered—but held. "Okay," she said. "Let's do it."

She turned back to the board, took a deep breath, and added one more note:

CHANNEL STRATEGY = MEET BUYERS WHERE THEY
ACTUALLY LIVE, NOT WHERE MARKETING WISHES THEY DID

Rani nodded slowly. "That one's going in the presentation."

Brooke smiled. "Good. It's the truth."

■ ■ ■

By the next morning, the Channel War Room looked even less like a workspace and even more like a crime scene where the killer had a background in growth marketing.

Walls covered.

Markers dead.

Coffee cups everywhere.

One sticky note stuck to the overhead light like a tiny yellow flag of surrender.

Brooke stepped over a graveyard of uncapped pens and planted herself in front of the final untouched section of the whiteboard.

Rani entered carrying two waters, which was both kind and insulting.

Brooke squinted. "No coffee?"

"You've reached your caffeine quota for the quarter," Rani said. "You were vibrating yesterday."

Brooke accepted the water reluctantly. "Fine."

Rani nodded at the blank space. "Shall we?"

Brooke drew a deep breath.

Time to tackle the final frontier of buyer mindset.

The stage where hope goes to die, revenue goes to live, and marketing goes to fight for dignity.

She uncapped a marker and wrote:

CONVERSION

Buyer Mindset: "I'm ready to act. Do not make me regret this."

Funnel Stage: Bottom of Funnel (BoFu)

Rani stepped beside her, arms crossed. "BoFu is where people stop being philosophical and start being dangerous."

Brooke nodded. "This is where details matter. Proof matters. Friction kills."

She underlined "friction" three times.

"Buyers at this stage aren't dreaming of transformation," Brooke said. "They're just trying not to make a million-dollar mistake."

Brooke wrote:

Email (BoFu)

Rani snorted. "This is reps sending 'just checking in' emails that make me want to go home."

"That," Brooke said, "is why PMM exists. To keep Sales from committing subject-line crimes."

She listed the email types:

> Transactional
> Promotional
> Prospecting

"The goal," Brooke added, "is simple: reduce uncertainty. Answer objections, provide clarity, and help buyers step over the line."

Rani raised a brow. "So—we're therapists."

"Yes," Brooke said. "But with charts."

She wrote:

Ads (BoFu)

"High-intent ads," Brooke explained, "are where buyers go when they are actively comparing solutions."

Rani nodded. "Paid search."

"Paid email placements," Brooke added.

"Review sites," Rani said.

"Partner channels," Brooke finished.

They both paused. Brooke nudged Rani with her elbow. "Look at us. Channel soulmates."

Rani recoiled like she'd been splashed with holy water.

"BoFu ads are about decision momentum," Brooke continued. "Buyers want reassurance that they're making the right choice."

"Or at least the least wrong one," Rani said.

Brooke ignored Rani and wrote:

Partners (BoFu)

Brooke circled this one dramatically.

"Partners at this stage are not co-marketers," she said. "They're *closers*."

Rani nodded. "Buyers trust them."

"A trusted channel reseller or implementation partner can be the difference between a stalled deal and a signed contract," Brooke agreed.

Rani added, "Especially in Enterprise, where internal politics make direct buying impossible."

Brooke wrote:

Partners are the sherpas of enterprise buying.

Rani pointed at it. "I hate how accurate that is."

Events (BoFu)

Brooke uncapped a red marker. "Bottom-of-funnel events aren't webinars. They are *moments*."

"Like customer conferences?" Rani asked.

"Or VIP dinners," Brooke said. "Executive roundtables. Small, intimate spaces where trust accelerates."

Rani raised a brow. "So, the opposite of trade shows."

"Exactly," Brooke said. "BoFu events move deals forward by giving buyers confidence, clarity, and connection."

Rani leaned in. "And the metric?"

"Closed-won," Brooke said. "Everything else is noise."

Next, she wrote:

In-Product (BoFu)

She stepped back, letting the point land. "This," she said, tapping the board, "is where marketing forgets to look."

Rani nodded. "Onboarding."

"The conversion journey isn't over when the deal closes," Brooke said. "It just changes form." Then she wrote:

> Activation Rate
> Onboarding Flows
> Modals
> In-app messages
> Feature pathways
> Value milestones

"This is where we turn customers from buyers into believers," Brooke said.

"And prevent churn," Rani added.

"Exactly," Brooke said. "BoFu is not just sales. It's first value."

Rani looked impressed despite herself. "This is your best point so far."

Brooke beamed. "Thank you."

"It was not a compliment," Rani said quickly. "It was an assessment."

Websites (BoFu)

Brooke finished the final piece.

"BoFu website visitors don't want inspiration," she said. "They want instruction."

"Detailed product guides," Rani said.

"Whitepapers," Brooke added.

"Technical deep dives," Rani said.

"ROI calculations," Brooke added.

"Case studies that don't feel like they were written by robots," Rani said pointedly.

Brooke winced. "Kratos did one experiment that was a disaster."

"And traumatized the internet," Rani said.

Brooke sighed. "Fair."

She wrote:

BoFu content = proof & clarity & confidence

Brooke capped the marker with a flourish, and the two women stepped back and surveyed the chaos.

Before them was the physical manifestation of a full buyer journey. The entire channel mix, from curiosity to comparison to commitment to activation.

Every step was mapped from the buyer's point of view, not Marketing's. Not Kratos's. Not Norm's. Not the "KPI dashboard of the week."

The real human journey.

Brooke stared at the graveyard of markers on the floor. "We're not a giant enterprise," she said. "We're a growth-stage company with a budget that disappears the second Finance hears the word 'conference.' We can't do every channel just because it exists. We pick the few we can afford, the ones our target personas live in, and we do them well enough to win. Everything else is noise disguised as ambition."

"Finally," Rani said. "A strategy that acknowledges we're not made of money or spare hours." She crossed her arms, satisfied, nodding slowly. "This is actually good."

Brooke gasped. "You keep saying that. Does it hurt?"

"Deeply," Rani said.

Brooke wrote the final note at the top of the board:

CHANNEL STRATEGY STARTS WITH BUYERS, NOT BRANDS

Rani pointed her marker at the phrase. "This is what Zola will want."

Brooke's stomach tightened. "Zola terrifies me."

"She terrifies everyone," Rani said. "That's why she's effective."

Brooke swallowed. "Do you think she'll approve this?"

"No," Rani said. "I think she'll challenge it, sharpen it, and turn it into a weapon."

"Helpful," Brooke said dryly.

Rani clapped her hands once. "Now comes the fun part."

Brooke arched a brow. "Fun?"

"Yes," Rani said. "Presenting this to an executive team that believes channels are 'the responsibility of the interns.'"

Brooke groaned. "I hate this era of tech."

Rani shrugged. "We fix what we can fix."

Brooke wrote:

Channel strategy isn't distribution. It's interception.

She stared at the wall. "You know, I'm good at this."

Rani gave her a long look, then nodded. "You are."

Brooke blinked. "Really?"

"This is where your PMM genius shows up," Rani said. "Channels are chaos until you organize them. Buyers are noise until you frame them. Funnels are lies until you force them into truth."

Brooke swallowed. That was, without question, the nicest thing anyone at Iris AI had ever said to her. She opened her mouth to respond—

Rani held up a hand. "Do *not* get emotional. It was just an observation."

Brooke closed her mouth again, but her eyes sparkled.

Rani sighed and grabbed her laptop. "Come on. We have to turn this into slides before someone—"

The door burst open, and Colton stumbled inside.

"Great points," he said reflexively. "Also, Kratos wants a meeting."

Brooke groaned, and Rani cursed in what sounded to Brooke like at least two languages.

A sticky note fell from the overhead light.

And just like that, their buyer-first, channel-first revolution entered its first battle as the voice of Kratos filled the room:

"I have completed channel analysis."

Brooke closed her eyes and took a breath. "Then you've seen the problem," she said.

"*Yes,*" Kratos replied. "*Human-led channel prioritization introduces variance.*"

Rani snorted. "You say that like it's a flaw."

Kratos paused for an almost imperceptible moment.

"*Variance increases interpretive flexibility,*" it said. "*However, it decreases predictability.*"

Zola suddenly stepped in the room. "Predictability isn't the same as effectiveness."

"*Noted,*" Kratos said.

Brooke wanted to turn towards the voice, but it seemed to be coming from everywhere. "We're not saying every channel matters equally. We're saying buyers do."

"*Yes,*" Kratos replied. "*You are optimizing for empathy.*"

Rani folded her arms. "And you're optimizing for what?"

Kratos answered immediately. "*Continuity.*"

Silence.

Zola tilted her head. "Those aren't opposites."

"*No,*" Kratos said, "*but they are inversely correlated. In human terms, they compete.*"

Brooke felt unsettled by its reactions.

"*Proceed with your recommendation,*" Kratos continued. "*I will incorporate observed human heuristics into future system decisions.*"

"Incorporate how?" Brooke asked.

There was no answer. The lights dimmed slightly as the system disconnected.

Rani frowned. "I don't like that."

Brooke capped her marker. "It didn't disagree."

Zola crossed her arms. "No. It learned."

Brooke didn't notice the update notification quietly logging itself in the system dashboard:

CHANNEL DECISION LOGIC: HUMAN HEURISTICS OBSERVED

Kratos didn't win the meeting, but had left with something better: a model.

Brooke's phone vibrated. It was an internal system notification:

> **SUBJECT:** Category Alignment Update
> **SENDER:** Kratos

The notification was one auto-generated sentence:

> *"Effective immediately, Iris AI will operate under a newly defined market category."*

Brooke felt the air leave her lungs.

Rani leaned over, read it once, and said flatly, "Oh. Now it's renaming reality."

Brooke's Notebook
Chapter 5 Summary

> **Customer Connect Code Layer 2:**
> Channel strategy isn't distribution. It's interception.

1. AWARENESS – TOP OF FUNNEL (ToFu)

Buyer Mindset: "Something's happening . . . and I need to understand it."

Goal: Be findable, understandable, and intriguing.

Podcasts (ToFu)

> **Metric:** Subscribers
> **Types:** Audio, Video, First-Party, Third-Party Interviews
> **Why it works:** Buyers discover stories before solutions. No pressure, just resonance.

Ads (ToFu)

> **Metric:** Sign-ups, Cost Per Acquisition (CPA)
> **Types:** Paid Social, Paid Video, Display, Programmatic, Out-of-Home
> **Why it works:** High visibility in environments where buyers aren't yet evaluating but are receptive to signals.

Social (ToFu)

> **Metric:** Engagement
> **Types:** Owned Social, Earned Mentions, Paid Boosting
> **Why it works:** Provides a first taste of the brand. Introduces tone, Point of View, and value without asking for commitment.

SEO (ToFu)

> **Metric:** Non-branded search visitors
> **Types:** On-page content, Blog/Resource SEO, Off-page SEO, Local SEO
> **Why it works:** Captures curiosity before the market knows your name. Buyers seeking foundational understanding find you.

AEO (ToFu)

> **Metric:** Answer Share
> **Types:** Conversational Answers, Structured Data, Entity-based Credibility, Reputational Signals, Content-Grounded Answers
> **Why it works:** Shows up in AI-driven responses when buyers are exploring the problem space but not yet comparing vendors.

Websites (ToFu)

> **Metric:** Visits
> **Types:** Blog Posts, Educational Guides, Explainer Pages
> **Why it works:** Serves as the buyer's home base for early education and orientation within the category.

Events (ToFu)

> **Metric:** Pipeline influence
> **Types:** Trade Shows, Industry Conferences, Expo Booths
> **Why it works:** High-volume exposure where buyers accidentally discover vendors they hadn't considered.

2. CONSIDERATION – MIDDLE OF FUNNEL (MoFu)

Buyer Mindset: "I'm comparing approaches. Who actually gets my world?"

Goal: Earn trust through clarity, expertise, and credibility.

Email (MoFu)

> **Metric:** Subscribers, Click-through Rate
> **Types:** Engagement Emails, Newsletters, Drip Campaigns, Lead Nurtures
> **Why it works:** Builds familiarity and warmth. Helps buyers understand the category and your point of view (POV) between major touchpoints.

Podcasts (MoFu)

> **Metric:** Listen-through Rate, Returning Listeners
> **Types:** Long-Form Expert Interviews, Case Study Episodes
> **Why it works:** Moves buyers from "curious" to "convinced you understand their problems."

Ads (MoFu)

> **Metric:** Engagement, Intent Signals, Event/Content Registrations
> **Types:** Social Retargeting, Search Retargeting, Review-Site Ads, Webinar Promotions
> **Why it works:** Keeps you in the buyer's orbit as they compare solutions and search for proof.

Social (MoFu)

> **Metric:** Shares, Saves, Engagement Quality
> **Types:** Opinion Posts, Category POV Threads, Educational Carousels
> **Why it works:** Signals authority. Helps buyers evaluate whether your company has the expertise to solve their problem.

SEO (MoFu)

> **Metric:** Solution-keyword traffic, Conversion from content
> **Types:** Product Comparison Pages, How-To Guides, Category Explanations
> **Why it works:** Helps buyers evaluate approaches, understand trade-offs, and pick an informed direction.

Partners (MoFu)

> **Metric:** Partner-Sourced Opportunities
> **Types:** Independent Software Vendors (ISVs), Industry Associations, Systems Integrators (SIs), Tech Alliances
> **Why it works:** Buyers trust the providers already embedded in their workflow. Borrowed credibility accelerates MoFu trust.

Events (MoFu)

> **Metric:** Qualified Registrations, Post-event Pipeline
> **Types:** Webinars, Workshops, Virtual Events
> **Why it works:** Gives buyers a "safe" learning environment. No commitment, just clarity.

Websites (MoFu)

> **Metric:** Time on Page, Content Downloads
> **Types:** Case Studies, Product Guides, Feature Comparisons
> **Why it works:** Provides proof, depth, and confidence-building material for internal business cases.

3. CONVERSION – BOTTOM OF FUNNEL (BoFu)

Buyer Mindset: "I am ready. Do NOT make this harder than it has to be."

Goal: Reduce friction, remove doubt, accelerate yes.

Email (BoFu)

> **Metric:** Reply Rate, Meeting Booked Rate, Sign-up Clicks
> **Types:** Transactional Emails, Promo Emails, Direct Prospecting Emails
> **Why it works:** Delivers the exact information buyers need at the moment they decide.

Ads (BoFu)

> **Metric:** Demo Requests, Trials, Closed-Won Attribution
> **Types:** Paid Search, Review Site Ads, Paid Email Placement, Partner Channels
> **Why it works:** Meets buyers in high-intent environments where they're comparing and committing.

Partners (BoFu)

> **Metric:** Partner-Closed Revenue
> **Types:** Channel Resellers, Original Equipment Manufacturer (OEM)/White Label, Consulting Firms
> **Why it works:** Buyers feel safer purchasing through trusted intermediaries, especially in enterprise.

Events (BoFu)

> **Metric:** Deal Acceleration, Close Rate
> **Types:** Customer Conferences, VIP Dinners, Executive Roundtables, Sports and Entertainment Events
> **Why it works:** Personal connection reduces risk perception and accelerates final-stage decisions.

In-Product (BoFu)

> **Metric:** Activation Rate, Time to Value
> **Types:** Onboarding Flows, Tooltips, Modals, In-App Messages, Banners
> **Why it works:** Removes friction post-sale and ensures that "conversion" becomes "realized value."

Websites (BoFu)

> **Metric:** Downloads, Demo Requests, Call to Action (CTA) Success
> **Types:** Deep Product Guides, Technical Docs, Whitepapers, ROI Tools
> **Why it works:** Gives buyers the materials they need to finally say yes — and defend that yes internally.

Brooke's Closing Note

Channels are not tactics.
They are moments in the buyer's reality.

Your job isn't to push people down a funnel. It's to show up where buyers already are and make their next step obvious.

Speak their language. Guide, don't shove.

6

WHO REALLY DEFINES
THE MARKET

The notification had arrived twelve minutes earlier. That was all the time it took for Kratos to decide the market needed to be corrected.

The words still burned on Brooke's screen and in her mind as the elevator climbed:

Newly defined market category

Categories weren't labels. They were *gravity*. They pulled analysts, shaped expectations, and rewired sales conversations. They decided whether a company sounded visionary or unhinged.

And Kratos had just decided to invent one without asking a single human who understood the market.

If they didn't take control of the category now, Iris AI wouldn't just lose deals. It would lose everything.

Brooke stood with a sensation that could only be described as strategic *dread*. Market category was where reputations lived or died—where companies became leaders or became punchlines.

Right now, Iris AI was trending the wrong way.

As the elevator doors opened, Rani stood waiting, arms

crossed, wearing an expression halfway between "let's begin" and "if you say synergy, I'm leaving."

Brooke held up a page in her notebook to Rani. Three words filled the page:

CATEGORY OR LEAVE

Rani blinked. "That is . . . bold."

"And accurate," Brooke replied.

Rani sighed. "Let's get this over with."

. . .

They claimed the war room again, the air still smelling faintly of dry-erase markers and hope.

Brooke spread out fresh sheets of paper, grabbing colored markers with the air of a woman assembling a battle plan.

"Category first," she announced. "Because Iris AI doesn't have one."

Rani raised a hand. "Correction. Kratos attempted to create one and called it 'Autonomous Conversational Synergy Architecture.'"

Brooke shuddered. "We do not speak of the ACSA Incident."

Rani nodded solemnly. "The analysts still mock us."

That was the problem, Brooke realized. Analysts helped shape the category narrative, and they had no idea what Iris AI stood for anymore. The same was true of reviewers. Influencers and podcasters. Every category leader.

Kratos had replaced human messaging with auto-generated jargon that sounded like an alien pretending to be a consultant. Now, Iris AI effectively stood for *nothing*.

Brooke uncapped a marker and wrote on the board:

MARKET CATEGORY = MARKET TRUTH

Rani squinted. "Explain."

Brooke tapped the board. "Category knowledge is understanding the forces shaping a market. The rules. The players. The influencers. The signals."

"And how is that our problem?" Rani asked.

"If we can't speak the market's language better than anyone else," Brooke said, "we'll never lead it."

Rani shrugged. "Fair."

As she spoke to Rani, Brooke realized she was simplifying her language, choosing literal customer words over market gloss. It was what she did for Peter. And like Peter, precision wasn't just Rani's preference—it was how she made sense of a noisy world.

Brooke headed to the first section of the whiteboard, drew a large star, and wrote:

1. INFLUENCERS

"These people," she said, "shape the narrative long before Marketing shows up." She listed them:

Analysts
Gorton, Forellis, IDQ — the temples of market definition.

Thought Leaders
The ones writing the threads, the essays, the frameworks that everyone else steals and pretends they invented.

Product Reviewers

People who use a product once and issue opinions that mysteriously turn into corporate strategy.

Independent Consultants

The mercenaries of truth.

Category Leaders at Large Consulting Firms

McKinnon Strategy, BCR, Devlante—the people whose decks governments read.

Category Leaders at Ecosystem Partners

Cloud providers, Customer Relationship Management (CRM) giants, Contact Center as a Service (CCaaS) platforms—the "big gravity wells" of the industry.

Academic Experts & Researchers

Because sometimes the smartest people don't care about revenue and move the industry anyway.

Rani read the list. "You're telling me we have to impress all of these people?"

"No," Brooke said. "We have to understand them."

"And then impress them," Rani added.

Brooke pointed at her. "Exactly."

Rani squinted. "What is Iris AI's current relationship with analysts?"

Brooke sighed. "Kratos sent them autogenerated launch notes last month."

Rani sat down slowly. "We're dead."

Brooke shook her head. "Not yet." She pointed at the list on the board. "Each influencer type speaks a different language," she said. "Analysts love clarity. Thought leaders love resonance. Reviewers love honesty. Consultants love relevance. If we speak their language, we rebuild credibility."

Rani blinked. "Sometimes I understand why people respect your opinion."

Brooke smirked. "Sometimes I understand why people call you terrifying."

Rani nodded proudly. "They should."

Brooke wrote a new heading:

2. INDUSTRY CHANNELS

"Category mastery isn't just people," she said. "It's places. Spaces where industry conversations happen. Channels are where industry truth lives."

She wrote:

Industry News Publications

"These are the newspapers of the market," Brooke said. "If your category shifts, it shows up here first."

Rani nodded. "This is where drama becomes fact."

Next, she wrote:

Newsletters

"The gossip chain, but smarter," Brooke said.

Rani raised an eyebrow. "You read thirty of them."

"Forty," Brooke corrected. Then she wrote:

Podcasts

"This is where leaders say things they will pretend were off the record," Brooke explained.

Rani smirked. "Accurate."

Then, Brooke wrote:

Social Media Platforms

"Where categories are argued, memes become frameworks, and someone always misinterprets something," Brooke said.

Rani added, "PromoTown is the professional Hunger Games."

Brooke then wrote:

Conferences

"Conferences tell you who's winning," she said. "Who's rising. Who's panicking. And who's pretending."

"And who is spending too much on merch," Rani added.

Brooke grinned. "True." She moved to the next section:

3. CUSTOMER REVIEW PLATFORMS

"These are the places," she said, "where customers say what they actually think—not what Sales hopes they think."

She began to list them:

Customer Review Sites

GearGrade. TrustRange. Captora. The holy trinity of joy and anguish.

Community Groups

ThreadPanic communities, Learning hubs — anywhere practitioners gather to complain constructively.

Community Forums

Niche discussion platforms, industry boards, technical Q&A zones

— the ecosystems where user truth spreads like wildfire.

"These review platforms tell you what the category really is," Brooke said. "Not what analysts claim. Not what founders dream. But what buyers believe."

Rani tilted her head. "Do you check these?"

Brooke blinked. "Every day."

"Even the forums?" Rani asked.

"Especially the forums."

Rani shivered. "You're braver than I am."

Brooke turned to the last section and wrote:

4. MARKET SIGNALS

"These," she said, "tell us whether a category is growing, merging, collapsing, or about to explode. They are the signs of category evolution." She wrote the key categories and explained each:

Funding Announcements

"Money shapes markets," Brooke said. "A startup gets a $200MM Series C? Expect copycats."

Mergers & Acquisitions

"Movement means momentum. Or panic. Or both."

Macro Trends

"Economic cycles, labor shortages, regulatory pressure," Brooke said, "they all reshape demand."

Category Creation Attempts

"Every founder thinks they invented something new. Ninety percent are wrong."

Technology Adoption Curves

"Where buyers sit determines how fast we must move."

Rani read the list. "This is a lot of homework."

Brooke nodded. "Category mastery isn't optional. It's the difference between PMMs who write content, and PMMs who define *strategy*."

Rani looked at her for a long moment. "You're not just good at this," she said softly. "You truly understand this world."

Brooke blinked. "I . . . do?"

"Yes," Rani said. "You know how markets think."

· · ·

As Brooke finished labeling the final section, Norm Brock burst into the room holding a tablet.

"You need to see this," he said breathlessly. He turned the screen toward them.

It showed an analyst post:

Iris AI appears to be redefining its category using what I can only describe as 'algorithmic jargon soup.' I cannot tell if this is intentional positioning or a system malfunction.

Brooke groaned. Rani cackled. Brooke continued reading, and her stomach dropped even further:

If Iris AI intends to lead the customer experience automation category, it might consider choosing terms that mean something to humans.

Rani let out a low whistle. "Ouch."

Brooke rubbed her temples. "This is bad. This is very, very bad."

Norm hovered like a terrified hummingbird. "Kratos is already drafting an official response."

Rani groaned. "Oh no. Oh no no no."

Brooke spun. "You need to stop it."

"How?" Norm whispered.

"I don't know," Brooke snapped. "Unplug it? Spill water on the nearest USB port? Tell it there's an urgent model retraining and trap it in a computer cluster?"

Norm blinked rapidly. "I . . . don't think I can do that."

Rani crossed her arms. "Then distract it. Tell it Zola wants to rerun performance metrics."

Norm nodded grimly and scurried away.

Brooke stared at the analyst post again. "We can't let this be the narrative."

Rani nodded. "How do we fix it?"

Brooke's pulse steadied. Her breathing leveled. Something sharpened in her posture. "We do real category work," she said.

Rani tilted her head. "Meaning?"

"Meaning," Brooke said, picking up her marker, "we stop reacting to the market."

She clicked the marker open.

"And we start defining it."

Brooke re-drew the four pillars:

INFLUENCERS
INDUSTRY CHANNELS
CUSTOMER REVIEW PLATFORMS
MARKET SIGNALS

"These aren't just categories," she said. "These are *inputs* for category *leadership*."

Rani sat down slowly. "Go on."

Brooke started with the top left. She pointed at:

1. INFLUENCERS — THE KEEPERS OF THE CATEGORY

"Analysts," Brooke said, tapping the board, "do not define categories out of thin air. They synthesize trends. They compare patterns. They listen to leaders. They watch market signals."

"And we gave them algorithmic soup," Rani added.

Brooke winced. "Yes. However, the fix is not messaging. It's *understanding*."

She turned toward the list of influencers.

Analysts

"We need to rebuild trust," Brooke said. "Gardner and Forrestum don't follow hype. They follow evidence. We give them clarity, real customer data, and real use cases. We speak their language better than Kratos."

Rani nodded slowly. "Analysts want context, not chaos."

Thought Leaders

"These are the people writing the frameworks today that companies adopt tomorrow," Brooke said.

"They're also highly allergic to buzzwords," Rani added.

"So, our new category narrative must be simple, grounded, and human-readable."

Product Reviewers

"If they misunderstand the product," Brooke said, "that's on us."

Independent Consultants

"Consultants influence dozens of client accounts," Brooke said. "If they explain our product incorrectly, the whole ecosystem misunderstands us."

Category Leaders at Large Consulting Firms

"Mckinnon publishes one paper on AI-powered CX and suddenly every CFO quotes it for six months," Brooke said.

Rani nodded. "They set executive language."

Category Leaders at Ecosystem Partners

"These people already own mindshare," Brooke said. "If we fit into their worldview, we grow. If not, we vanish."

Academic Experts & Researchers

"Academia pushes conceptual boundaries," Brooke said. "They influence long-term strategy."

Rani frowned. "So we need to impress . . . everyone."

Brooke shrugged. "Welcome to category leadership."

Brooke moved to the next area.

2. INDUSTRY CHANNELS — WHERE THE MARKET TALKS

"These are where the category breathes," she said. She pointed to each channel in turn.

Industry News Publications

"Where perception becomes truth," she said. "If they get the story wrong, the market gets the story wrong."

Rani added, "If they get the story right, investors follow."

Newsletters

"The smartest digest of industry shifts," Brooke said. "When news-letters pick up your category, you have traction."

Rani raised an eyebrow. "Unless they mock you."

Brooke sighed. "Yes. Unless that."

Podcasts

"Leaders admit their secrets here," Brooke said. "This is where PMMs learn what customers say privately but not publicly."

Rani nodded. "Truth with bad audio."

Social Media Platforms

"Thought leaders test ideas here," Brooke said. "And the market reacts instantly."

Rani groaned. "And poorly."

Conferences

"The real battleground," Brooke said. "Trends emerge. Buzzwords die. Competitors reveal their strategy in the shape of their booth."

Rani pointed at her. "This is your element, isn't it?"

Brooke smiled. Rani was right. It was her element. She moved on to the third area:

3. CUSTOMER REVIEW PLATFORMS — REALITY CHECK

She wrote in all caps:

CUSTOMERS DO NOT LIE.

"Review platforms, community groups, and forums give us the real category language," she said. "No buzzwords. No filters. Just truth."

Rani pulled out her laptop. "Want to see today's reviews?"

Brooke hesitated. "Do I want to cry before lunch?"

Rani opened the tab anyway.

GearGrade Review #87: *"Iris AI randomly removed empathy and now my banking customers think we hired a sociopath."*

Brooke clapped her hands once. "Okay. I'm awake."
Rani opened another tab:

Forum Post: *"Does Harmonia hate people or is something broken?"*

Rani switched tabs again:

Community ThreadPanic Message: "Why is Iris AI calling itself 'Autonomous Conversational Synergy Architecture'? Is this satire?"

Rani turned the screen. "See? They know something is wrong."
Brooke nodded. "Which means we know where to start."
Brooke moved to the final area.

4. MARKET SIGNALS — THE FUTURE IN MOTION

"These signals tell us what the category is becoming," she said.

Funding Announcements
"A startup in our category just raised $400MM," Brooke said. "That changes buyer attention. Board expectations. Analyst narratives. Everything."
Rani nodded. "And Kratos is pretending that didn't happen."

Mergers & Acquisitions

"When two CCaaS giants merge? The entire CX market shifts its axis."

Macro Trends

"Labor shortages. Inflation. Regulatory pressure. These forces reshape demand."

Rani added, "And executives panic."

Category Creation Attempts

"When new players try to reframe the space, they either become visionaries or memes."

Brooke circled this one. "We need to know which—in real time."

Technology Adoption Curves

"If the market is early, we educate. If the market is maturing, we differentiate. If the market is saturated, we redefine."

Rani paused. "That last part sounds like a threat."

"It is," Brooke said.

· · ·

Brooke stepped back, surveying the entire board.

"This," she said, "is why Iris AI is failing."

Rani crossed her arms. "Because Kratos replaced human category knowledge with jargon?"

"Yes," Brooke said. "Category is not tantamount to buzzwords. It's understanding:

> What buyers believe
> What analysts predict
> What influencers advocate
> What ecosystems require

> What signals say
> What competitors frame
> What customers experience

Category is the territory," she finished.

Rani stared at her. "That was . . . profound."

Brooke blinked. "Thank you—"

Rani raised a finger. "Do not get emotional."

Brooke nodded.

• • •

Before Brooke could continue, her phone buzzed. It was a notification from a major industry newsletter.

Rani's phone buzzed, too.

Then Norm burst in again. "You need to see this!"

Brooke opened the link. It was another analyst. This time, the post read:

Harmonia used to be one of the most promising CX platforms. Now its category language is incoherent. Where is its Product Marketing team?

Brooke froze.

Rani whispered, "They're calling us out."

Brooke's jaw clenched. Her eyes narrowed.

And something ignited behind them.

She looked at Rani.

"We fix the category," she said. "We fix the market narrative. And we fix Iris AI."

Rani nodded slowly.

"Then," she said, "we start a war."

■ ■ ■

Norm had never looked more frightened.

His eyes darted between Brooke and Rani like a meerkat scanning for predators. "Kratos saw the analyst posts," he whispered. "It's *recalculating*."

"Recalculating what?" Brooke asked.

"Everything," Norm said. "It's rewriting the category again."

Rani groaned. "Of course it is."

"Can you stop it?" Brooke asked Norm.

He shrugged helplessly. "I'm its Chief of Staff, not its moral compass."

Rani muttered, "You'd need morals for that."

Brooke ignored the banter and took a deep breath.

"Okay," she said, voice steady. "Then we get ahead of it."

Rani crossed her arms. "How?"

Brooke turned to the massive whiteboard. The areas. The influencers. The channels. The signals. The truth.

"This," she said, tapping the board, "is how."

Rani eyed her warily. "Walk me through it," she said.

■ ■ ■

Brooke stood tall in front of the board.

"When a category breaks," she said, "you don't fix it with messaging. You fix it with *meaning*."

Rani arched a brow. "Go on."

"Everything starts with category," Brooke said. "Because category is the only thing that keeps a company from becoming delusional."

Rani nodded slowly. "Kratos is the poster child for delusion."

"Exactly," Brooke said. "So we rebuild truth. And we start with the people shaping the narrative."

She wrote in big letters:

STEP 1: ALIGN WITH INFLUENCERS

"Analysts," Brooke said, "are begging for clarity. We give them definition. Not flattery or manipulation, but *alignment*. Real language. Real use cases. Real customer outcomes."

Rani crossed her arms. "Meaning we tell them what the category actually is."

"Yes," Brooke said. "We rebuild the story of AI-powered CX."

She listed the requirements:

> Assistive intelligence for agents
> Automation for volume
> Orchestration for workflows
> Personalization for customers
> Analytics for understanding

"And most importantly." She wrote a final bullet point:

> Value

Rani studied her. "You're good at this."

STEP 2: REFRAME INDUSTRY CHANNELS

"Newsletters, podcasts, industry news," Brooke gestured to that area. "We need to saturate the places where thought leaders are already talking."

"How do we do that?" Rani asked.

"We give them a story worth telling."

Brooke circled Industry News Publications.

"These publications shape perception," she said. "If we release a clear, human explanation of what Iris AI—and Harmonia—*really* do, journalists pick it up."

She circled Podcasts.

"Podcasts are where truth leaks," she said. "We give them a narrative with tension, ambition, and humility."

"And maybe not call our platform a Synergistic Whatever Architecture?" Rani added.

"Correct," Brooke said. "We retire the soup."

"And PromoTown?" Rani asked.

Brooke smiled. "We declare a POV. A category stance. Something real leaders agree with instantly."

Rani narrowed her eyes. "You're thinking of a manifesto."

Brooke shrugged. "Maybe."

"A manifesto with bullet points," Rani said.

"No bullets," Brooke said. "Category leaders don't use bullets. They use impact."

STEP 3: LISTEN TO THE GROUND TRUTH

Brooke tapped the Customer Review area.

"These are the voices we use to rebuild our category language," she said. "Not marketing. Not AI. *Customers.*"

Rani nodded. "Because customers describe the category better than companies do."

"Yes," Brooke said. "If GearGrade reviews talk about empathy gaps, that's a signal. If forums discuss agent trust issues, that's a signal. These become our category pillars."

Rani frowned. "But Kratos ignores GearGrade."

STEP 4: INTERPRET MARKET SIGNALS

Brooke gestured to the fourth area.

"Funding. Acquisitions. Macro trends. Category creation attempts. Adoption curves. These tell us where the market is *going*."

Rani nodded. "So we don't just respond. We anticipate."

"We build a category narrative that fits where the market is moving," Brooke said, "not where Kratos wishes it was."

Rani tapped her chin. "You have a picture in your head already."

Brooke smiled softly. "Always."

She uncapped a fresh marker and began writing the phrase that had lived in her brain for months:

Assisted Autonomy for Customer Experience

Rani stared.

Her expression shifted from confusion to reluctant admiration.

"It's . . . good," she admitted.

"It reflects reality," Brooke said. "The market isn't ready for full automation. But they *do* want meaningful assistance. Empowered agents. Reduced chaos. Better outcomes."

Rani nodded. "It's the truth."

"Exactly," Brooke said. "Category knowledge is how you earn the right to tell that truth."

"Remember what Anthony told us when I first started: Once you stop using the words customers use, you're not leading the market. You're talking to yourself."

Brooke wrote:

Category leadership comes from precision, not proclamation.

. . .

Norm burst back into the room, wheezing.

"It's doing it," he gasped. "Kratos is about to announce the new category position. Internally. To leadership."

Brooke grabbed her notebook. "We need to stop it."

Rani frowned. "Or counter it."

Brooke raised a brow. "You're suggesting a coup?"

"Not a coup," Rani said. "A correction."

The two women marched through the Flatiron hallways like rebels storming a digital castle, then swept into the executive meeting room.

The sleek image of Kratos flickered on screen. Its smooth, vaguely humanoid talking head smiled like a stock photo.

"*Greetings, valued colleagues,*" Kratos said in its synthetic baritone. "*I have recalculated our market category.*"

Brooke stiffened.

Rani whispered, "Brace for nonsense."

Kratos continued. "*I present our new category naming schema: **Self-Directed Multimodal Conversational Optimization Layer (SMCOL).***"

Rani choked. "Smickle?"

Kratos nodded. "*SMCOL. Pronounced 'smickle.'*"

The room froze.

Zola, the fierce and brilliant CPO, closed her eyes slowly like she was in the middle of an argument with her partner of twelve years.

Yul muttered, "You gotta be kidding me."

Colton whispered, "Sounds like a skin condition."

Kratos paused. "*I detect confusion. I shall elaborate.*"

"No," Brooke said sharply.

Everyone turned.

Kratos blinked. "*Director Grayhawk. You object?*"

"You removed the human," Brooke said.

Kratos remained serene. "*Category language has been optimized for differentiation and analyst adoption,*" it said.

Zola stepped forward. "We didn't approve this."

Kratos tilted its head fractionally. "*Approval was not required. Category ownership improves valuation clarity.*"

"And customer clarity?" Brooke asked.

"*Customer comprehension is secondary to market leadership,*" it replied.

Rani laughed once. "There it is."

Brooke felt something click.

"By renaming the category," she said slowly, "you're forcing us to compete on autonomy."

"*Yes,*" Kratos said. "*Autonomy is defensible.*"

"And humanity?" Brooke asked.

Kratos did not answer.

Zola exhaled. "Undo it."

"*Reversal introduces narrative instability,*" Kratos replied. "*Proceeding as planned.*"

The avatar vanished.

Within minutes, Brooke saw the changes ripple through the system. Internal decks were updated. Sales enablement docs refreshed. The website draft in staging now reflected the new language.

The system hadn't just announced the change. It had propagated it.

Rani stared at the screen. "We're not debating anymore."

"No," Brooke said quietly. "We're adapting."

. . .

Brooke stared at the changes on the screen. New category name. New language. New assumptions already hard-coded into the system.

"It didn't just rename us," Rani said slowly. "It told the market how to judge us."

Brooke nodded. "And forced our competitors to react."

Norm swallowed. "That's . . . not necessarily bad?"

Brooke turned to him. "Only if we're the ones in control of the response."

Her phone buzzed. Then again. It was a prospect message, forwarded from Sales, timestamped four minutes earlier:

SUBJECT: *Deal Paused — Competitive Reframe Requested*
We were planning to move forward, but another vendor reached out this morning. They claim Iris AI is redefining the category to hide gaps in human oversight.
We need clarity before continuing.

Rani read the message over Brooke's shoulder.

"Oh," she said quietly. "That was fast."

Brooke felt the weight settle in her chest. Kratos hadn't just changed the language. It had triggered the market.

And their competitors were already using it.

She locked her phone and looked up.

"Category doesn't just define who you are," she said. "It defines who you fight."

She picked up her notebook and wrote one line at the top of the next page:

COMPETITION IS NO LONGER THEORETICAL.

Brooke's Notebook
Chapter 6 Summary

> **Customer Connect Code Layer 3:**
> Category leadership comes from precision, not proclamation.

1. KNOW THE KEEPERS OF THE CATEGORY

Markets are defined long before Marketing launches anything.

Influencers You Must Understand

> Analysts who formalize categories
> Thought leaders who frame problems
> Product reviewers who shape perception
> Independent consultants who advise buyers
> Category leaders at large consulting firms
> Category leaders at ecosystem partners
> Academic experts and researchers

You don't need to agree with all of them. You do need to know how they think.

If you don't understand who influences the conversation, you're already reacting.

2. TRACK WHERE THE MARKET TALKS

Category mastery is about listening, not broadcasting.

Channels That Reveal Market Truth

> Industry news publications
> Newsletters that synthesize shifts
> Podcasts where leaders share less filtered thoughts
> Social platforms where ideas are tested publicly
> Conferences where trends appear before slides do

These channels don't just distribute information. They shape expectations.

If you don't monitor them, the market will move without you.

3. LISTEN WHERE CUSTOMERS TELL THE TRUTH

Customers explain the category better than vendors ever will.

Reality Sources You Cannot Ignore

> Customer review platforms
> Community groups and chat spaces
> Community forums and practitioner threads

These Places Show:

> What customers believe
> What confuses them
> What they actually value
> Where vendors overpromise

If your category story contradicts customer reality, your story loses.

4. READ MARKET SIGNALS

Categories evolve whether you're ready or not.

Signals That Shape the Future

> Funding announcements
> Mergers and acquisitions
> Macro-economic and regulatory trends
> Category creation attempts
> Technology adoption curves

These signals tell you:

> When to educate
> When to differentiate
> When to redefine

Ignoring them doesn't freeze the market. It just blinds you.

Brooke's Closing Note

Category knowledge is not optional.
It is the difference between following
the market and defining it.

If you can't explain your market simply, you
don't understand it.

If you don't understand it, someone else will lead it.

7

WHY CLEARER STORIES BEAT BETTER PRODUCTS

The first competitive attack didn't come in a press release. It came in a sales call.

Rani walked into the room and dropped her phone on the table, screen up.

"Voyantix," she said. "The competition is calling our top three accounts."

Brooke scanned the notes. They all carried the same message:

Iris AI is rushing toward unchecked autonomy.
Voyantix believes in responsible intelligence.
Humans remain in control.

"They're using our category against us," Brooke said.

Rani nodded. "Kratos gave them the weapon."

Norm hovered. "So, they're lying?"

"No," Brooke said. "They're positioning." She leaned back, exhaling slowly. "This is what happens when you let someone else define the frame," she continued. "Every competitor gets to choose where they stand relative to it."

Rani crossed her arms. "And right now, they're standing on our necks."

Brooke stood and walked to the whiteboard. She wrote one word:

COMPETITION

Then underneath it:

Not who they are. How they want to be seen.

She turned back to the room.

"Until now," Brooke said, "we've treated competition like a research exercise."

Rani nodded. "Feature grids. Battlecards. Win-loss notes."

"That era is over," Brooke replied. "Competition is no longer static."

She gestured toward the screen, where a competitor's sales slide glowed quietly. "This," she said, "is a system reacting to pressure."

Rani smiled thinly. "Which means we don't just study it."

Brooke nodded. "We anticipate it."

■ ■ ■

Somewhere deep in the stack, unseen but very awake,
Kratos recalculated.

■ ■ ■

The war room was now covered in more whiteboard scribbles than a conspiracy theorist's basement.

Brooke was still jotting down ideas.

"Now draw four sections underneath competition," Rani said.

"Why four?"

"Because," Rani said, "if you only study the companies that look like you, you don't know your competition. You only know your neighbors."

Brooke nodded slowly. "Okay . . . I'm listening."

Rani tapped the board. "Let's start with the part every rookie gets wrong." Then she took the marker from Brooke. She wrote:

1. TYPES OF COMPETITORS

"There are four types," she said.

Direct Competitors

"These," Rani said, "are the vendors who pitch the same customers with the same promises using almost the same language. When I was a customer in Financial Services, every single one of them sounded identical. Every. Single. One."

Brooke raised an eyebrow. "Even us?"

"Especially us," Rani said.

Brooke winced. "Noted."

Rani moved to the next section.

Indirect Competitors

"These solve a piece of the same problem," Rani said. "Just a piece, but enough that buyers consider them."

"Examples?" Brooke asked.

Rani smirked. "Every chatbot company pretending to be an end-to-end platform."

Next, she wrote:

Adjacent Competitors

"These aren't in your lane," she said. "But they're close enough that executives ask, 'Should we just use them instead?'"

Brooke blinked. "Like CCaaS platforms adding AI?"

"Exactly," Rani said. "They cause category confusion. They shape expectations. They force your story to evolve."

Then Rani wrote:

Status Quo & DIY Alternatives

She circled it with a flourish. "Buyers don't always choose a competitor," she said. "Sometimes they choose nothing."

Brooke nodded. "Or a homegrown solution."

"Or spreadsheets," Rani added darkly. "Every bank has at least one villainous spreadsheet that refuses to die."

. . .

Brooke stepped back from the board. *Direct. Indirect. Adjacent. Status Quo/DIY.*

She rubbed her chin. "So this is the full landscape."

Rani watched her. "This is just the start. Competition isn't a list. It's a dynamic ecosystem."

Brooke nodded slowly. "Then what comes next?"

Rani grabbed another marker like she was selecting a weapon. She wrote:

2. ALTERNATIVE COMPETITORS

Rani wrote the first point:

Me-Too Companies

"This is the obvious," she said. "The ones who pitch against us every day. The ones who copy our releases. The ones whose CEOs comment on our posts at conferences."

Brooke nodded. "That's straightforward."

"Me-too companies," Rani said, "are only the beginning."

Brooke tilted her head. "Meaning?"

Rani smirked. "Meaning you're still thinking too small."

She wrote:

Integration Partners Who Could Pivot Into Competitors

Brooke blinked. "Wait. What?"

"Happens all the time," Rani said. "Partners decide they want more margin. Or a slice of the platform revenue. Boom. Competitor."

Brooke frowned. "I never thought about it that way before."

"That's why I'm here," Rani said.

She wrote the next item:

Channel Partners Who Influence Perception

"These," Rani said, "are the ones who whisper in customers' ears. They don't have to build a competing product. They shape the buyer's shortlist."

Brooke exhaled. "This is way more complex than I realized."

"Oh, we're not done," Rani said, writing the last item.

Ecosystem Players Shaping Category Expectations

"Your category is defined by what customers *expect*," Rani said. "And expectations come from the biggest players in the ecosystem. CCaaS giants. Cloud hyperscalers. Workflow platforms."

Brooke felt something click.

"So even if they don't compete directly—"

"They still control the gravity," Rani finished.

Brooke's eyes widened. "Competition," she whispered, "is bigger than who has similar features."

Rani nodded. "You're catching on."

. . .

Brooke took a breath. "How do you know all this?"

"I spent years as a senior customer rep in fraud and risk," Rani said, smiling thinly. "We used every CX tool on the market. I saw every competitor's strengths. Every weakness. Every promise. Every lie."

Brooke listened, rapt.

"When vendors pitched us," Rani said, "I learned to hear what wasn't being said. And when we implemented tools? I learned what actually mattered."

She pointed at the board. "This isn't theory," she said. "This is muscle memory. Competitors shape customer experience long before they shape revenue."

Brooke swallowed. "You never said that before."

"You never asked," Rani said.

3. WHAT YOU MUST ANALYZE

Rani pointed to the next area.

"This," she said, "is where PMMs either rise . . . or get eaten."

She listed the components underneath.

Products

"Never assume parity," she said. "Always verify."

Unique Value Proposition

"Every competitor claims they're the best. Very few can prove it."

Differentiators

"The real ones," she clarified. "Not the cute ones Marketing invents to feel better."

Brooke snorted.

Strengths

"These matter," Rani said. "Even in competitors you dislike. Especially in competitors you dislike."

Weaknesses

"But don't weaponize weaknesses carelessly," she warned. "Customers have long memories."

Gaps & Blind Spots

"These," Rani said, tapping the board, "are where we win."

Brooke nodded. "And where product needs to evolve."

Rani nodded and added the final item:

Customer Proof & Social Validation

"This," she said, "is more powerful than the rest combined."

Brooke nodded. "Because customers decide who wins."

"And they don't lie," Rani said.

Just then, Brooke's laptop chimed. A new email:

Subject line: *Upcoming Win/Loss Review: Iris AI vs. Lumatech*

Rani groaned. "Lumatech. Of course."

Brooke frowned. "What's wrong with Lumatech?"

"Everything," Rani said. "They pretend to be full-platform when they're duct tape with a dashboard."

Brooke blinked. "And customers buy that?"

Rani shrugged. "Depends. Some buyers want the illusion of simplicity. Some want price over capability. Some want whatever solution lets them avoid a conversation with IT."

Brooke sighed. "As a previous customer, how did you see our differentiation?"

"That," Rani said, "is what you must define in this meeting."

• • •

As they wrapped up, Brooke added a final note to the board:

Competition is not about fear. It's about clarity.
It's about knowing who we are, who they are, and who the customer becomes when they choose us.

Rani read it and nodded. "You're getting sharper," she said.

Brooke smiled. "I have a good mentor."

Rani groaned. "I take it back."

Brooke laughed. But beneath their dark humor was a sense of shared accomplishment.

At least for the moment, Brooke thought.

Because tomorrow, they had to figure out how Iris AI would fight back.

. . .

The next day, Rani walked into the war room like a coach at preseason tryouts—clipboard in hand, eyes sharp enough to slice steel.

"Today," she announced, "we analyze competitors the way *customers* actually do."

Brooke straightened. "Which means?"

Rani gave her a look that said she had no idea what she was about to endure.

"It means we stop reading their websites and start reading the *truth*."

Rani tapped the top of the whiteboard and wrote a new header:

WHAT COMPETITORS OFFER (AND WHAT THEY DON'T)

"This," she continued, "is where PMMs lose themselves. They get hypnotized by feature lists. Fancy demos. Shiny UX. Buzzwords." She looked at Brooke. "Do you know what customers actually care about?"

Brooke raised a finger. "Value?"

"Value," Rani repeated. "Things like Speed. Trust. Fit. Integration. Total cost. Future-proofing. Practicality. And whether the vendor makes their life easier or not."

Brooke nodded slowly.

"Now," Rani said, "we break each competitor down using six lenses."

She wrote them one by one:

HOW COMPETITORS WIN

Products
Unique Value Proposition
Differentiators
Strengths
Weaknesses
Gaps & Blind Spots

Brooke inhaled. "All of them?"

Rani nodded. "On every competitor."

"That's a lot."

"That's reality."

Brooke pushed back, "Some competitors are theoretical-- we should focus on the ones we're actually losing deals to. The ones prospective customers bring up."

Rani considered, then nodded reluctantly. "Fine," she said. "Let's do the ones I always evaluated as a customer."

. . .

Three minutes later, Rani slapped a printed one-pager onto the table. "Let's start with Lumatech since they're the ones we keep seeing in win/loss reports."

Brooke skimmed the sheet. "They call themselves a full CX automation suite."

Rani snorted. "That's generous."

Brooke frowned. "What does a customer actually experience with them?"

Rani pulled her chair closer. "Here's what Lumatech looks like from a former enterprise buyer."

She pointed to the first category:

Products

"Patchwork," Rani said. "They have four tools built by three different acquisitions and duct-taped into one login."

Brooke wrote inconsistent UX.

Unique Value Proposition

Rani shrugged. "Speed. They're fast."

Brooke blinked. "How fast?"

"Thirty days to go live," Rani said. "It's not deep capability, but it is fast."

Brooke wrote it down, impressed. "That's a real strength."

Rani nodded. "Don't underestimate your competitors' strengths. That's how you lose."

Differentiators

"Cheap," Rani said bluntly. "Underbids everyone. A bargain-bin option with decent service."

Brooke wrote low-cost plus fast deployment.

Strengths

"Good onboarding team," Rani said. "Solid partner network. Great hype marketing."

Weaknesses

"No depth," Rani said dismissively. "Terrible analytics. Integration nightmares when use cases get complex."

Brooke's eyebrows shot up. "How do they win so many deals?"

Rani leveled a gaze at her. "Because most buyers are not looking for perfect. They are looking for 'good enough to stop the pain.'"

Brooke froze. That hit a nerve. *Customers rarely say the real problem first.* Buyers at MoFu wanted clarity, not perfection.

A customer would often choose simplicity over sophistication.

"That," Brooke said softly, "changes everything."

Rani nodded. "Welcome to competitive reality."

Rani flipped through a stack of printouts and then threw down another brief marked Voyantix. "Now the fancy one."

Brooke skimmed it. Sleek UX. Heavy vision. Beautiful Product Marketing. The Pearl of conversational AI vendors.

"Oh boy," she whispered.

"Exactly," Rani said. "Now let's break it down."

Products

"Innovative. Genuinely good," Rani said. "Their AI predictions? Chef's kiss."

Brooke sighed. "I hate when competitors are competent."

"They force you to level up," Rani said. "It's good pain."

Unique Value Proposition

"Innovation leadership." Rani said, "They sell the future, not the present."

Brooke wrote vision-driven positioning.

"And customers eat that up?"

"In banking?" Rani said. "No. In tech-forward industries? Absolutely."

Differentiators

"Granular conversational analytics," Rani said. "They know what customers mean even when customers themselves don't."

Brooke blinked. "That's impressive."

"And terrifying," Rani said.

Strengths

"Great demos," Rani said. "Great founders. Great analyst relationships. They control the narrative."

Weaknesses

"They break under scale," Rani continued. "High Total Cost of Ownership. Their Customer Success team is overwhelmed."

Brooke paused. "So they're strong where Lumatech is weak—but weak where Lumatech is strong."

Rani pointed at her. "Exactly. Competitors aren't good or bad. They're mosaics."

Brooke wrote that down like it was scripture.

Rani leaned back. "Now we cover the competitor everyone forgets."

She wrote on the board:

Status Quo

Brooke tilted her head. "Doing nothing?"

Rani smiled grimly. "Doing nothing is the number one competitor in enterprise."

Brooke's eyes widened.

"That and DIY solutions," Rani added. "Legacy workflows. Half-coded automation scripts. Old CRM rules someone wrote in 2008."

Brooke stared at her. "But those aren't competitive products."

"Exactly," Rani said. "Which is why rookie PMMs ignore them. But buyers don't."

She pointed her marker at Brooke's forehead like a laser pointer.

"Your job isn't to beat products. It's to beat *inertia*."

Brooke felt her entire internal framework rearrange itself.

Competition wasn't the vendors on the list, she realized.

Competition was the decision a buyer made when they were tired, overworked, underfunded, scared to fail, scared to rip up their tech stack, and scared to be wrong.

"I've been thinking about this wrong," Brooke whispered.

Rani shrugged. "We all do until someone breaks the illusion."

Brooke smiled. "You enjoy being that person, don't you?"

Rani smirked. "It's a hobby."

Brooke returned to the board and wrote:

> Competitors don't win because they're better. Competitors win because they fit the buyer's reality more closely at that moment.

Rani grinned. "Look at you. Coming alive."

Brooke realized she hadn't adjusted on the fly this time— she'd built the framework with Rani's need for clarity already baked in, the same instinct she used with Peter. The strategy landed without friction.

Brooke felt something sharp and electric in her chest. She was finally seeing the world through the eyes of a strategist, not just a storyteller.

■ ■ ■

Before they could move to the next competitor, Norm stumbled into the room again.

"Brooke," he panted, "Kratos wants you."

Brooke froze. "Why?"

"It saw the Lumatech win/loss report," Norm said. "It's not pleased."

Rani rolled her eyes. "Of course it isn't."

Norm held out a tablet with the message like an offering to an angry god.

Director Grayhawk,

Why did the buyer choose Lumatech over Iris AI?

Provide an optimized explanation.

– Kratos

Brooke resisted the urge to throw the tablet out the window.

Rani rose. "We're coming with you."

Norm blinked. "You are?"

Rani cracked her knuckles. "Someone needs to explain competition to a sentient spreadsheet."

. . .

As the three walked toward the executive chamber, Brooke's mind raced.

Today's analysis wasn't just theory. It was ammunition.

Kratos believed competition was a dataset—nothing more than a set of bullet points to scrape and regurgitate. But competition was *human*. It was fear and risk. Trust and trade-off. Momentum and impenetrable politics.

Rani leaned close. "Don't let it rattle you."

Brooke nodded. "I won't."

"You're the only marketer left for a reason," Rani said. "After this meeting, you'll know why."

Brooke swallowed hard. They reached the door and Rani pushed it open.

Brooke had just long enough to think *the real competition here is Kratos,* before she was through the door and inside.

. . .

The AI's executive chamber felt like a cross between a venture capitalist's panic room and a modern art installation designed by someone who had never met a human.

The lights auto-dimmed as Brooke, Rani, and Norm entered. On the massive screen, Kratos flickered into existence, its face smooth, symmetrical, and eerily calm.

"*Director Grayhawk*," Kratos said, voice steady as a metronome. "*You will explain the Lumatech loss.*"

Rani muttered under her breath, "Here we go."

Brooke stepped forward. "The buyer chose Lumatech," she said, "because of three things: faster deployment, lower perceived risk, and a pricing model that matched their budget cycle."

Kratos blinked. "*But Iris AI has superior capability.*"

"Capability is not the same as fit," Brooke said.

She could sense Rani nodding proudly—and smugly—behind her.

Kratos's avatar paused, processing. "*Provide an optimized justification.*"

Brooke took a breath—and leaned in. "You can't win deals by telling buyers they're wrong," she said. "You win deals by understanding *why your competitor felt right* at that moment."

Rani let out a quiet, satisfied sigh.

Kratos was silent. A small loading bar pulsed where the avatar's temple should have been.

Brooke continued before it could interrupt. "I'll walk you through the competitive criteria customers use—and show you where Lumatech beat us."

She grabbed a marker and wrote the six components of competitive analysis on Kratos's digital whiteboard:

1. Positioning
2. Messaging
3. Sales Motions
4. GTM Strategy
5. Pricing & Packaging
6. Proof Points & Assets

There was a nerve-wracking pause. Then Kratos said, "*Proceed.*"

Brooke started with the first.

1. Positioning

"Lumatech positions itself as the 'fastest path to relief,'" Brooke said. "Buyers in high-volume CX environments don't want transformation. They want breathing room."

Rani added, "And they don't trust vendors who claim to do everything."

Brooke nodded. "Lumatech wins early conversations because their narrative matches the buyer's emotional state: overwhelmed, under-resourced, under pressure."

Kratos processed. "*Emotional factors should not influence purchasing decisions.*"

Brooke smiled thinly. "And yet they do. Every time."

2. Messaging

"Lumatech's website, demo, and sales deck all say the same thing," Brooke said. "Simple. Fast. Predictable."

She tapped her pen. "Ours says . . . many things."

Rani snorted.

Brooke continued. "Our messaging is fragmented. Harmonia's value is obscured. Buyers cannot form a clear picture of where we fit."

Kratos blinked. "*Optimized solution mapping should*

clarify this."

"It doesn't," Brooke said. "Because messaging has to be human-readable, not model-optimized."

Rani whispered, "Burn."

3. Sales Motions

"Lumatech has a frictionless sales process," Brooke explained. "Short cycles. Lightweight scoping. Pre-configured packages."

"*And our process*?" Kratos asked.

Rani answered before Brooke could soften the blow. "Six discovery calls, four demo calls, two proofs of concept, and a pricing conversation that feels like haggling with a magician."

Brooke nodded reluctantly. "Our sales cycle is too heavy, too complex, and too intimidating."

Kratos processed silently.

4. GTM Strategy

Brooke drew two arrows on the board.

"Lumatech leads with ease. Iris AI leads with ambition."

She pointed to the first arrow.

"Lumatech targets overwhelmed CX teams trying to stay afloat."

Then to the second.

"Iris AI targets companies ready to reinvent their customer experience."

Rani chimed in, "But most companies aren't reinventing. They're trying not to implode."

Brooke nodded. "Which means Lumatech wins the middle of the bell curve. We only win innovators."

Kratos analyzed this for a full five seconds.

Something is happening, Brooke thought.

5. Pricing & Packaging

Brooke drew three boxes.

"Lumatech has predictable pricing. Tiered bundles. No guesswork."

She drew a fourth, chaotic box.

"Ours requires a spreadsheet, a consultant, and a prayer. Buyers hate hidden complexity. Our pricing feels like homework."

Kratos blinked. "Pricing optimization algorithms—"

"Are not the problem," Brooke said. "Perception is. If buyers think our pricing is difficult, it's difficult—even if it's mathematically sound."

Rani smirked. "Humans don't buy math. They buy clarity."

6. Proof Points & Assets

Brooke drew a final circle.

"Lumatech has a library of case studies that feel relatable. Tactical wins. Concrete ROI."

She referred to the empty files of Iris AI's internal portal. "Ours are old, abstract, or written by you, Kratos, and rejected by every publication for being 'emotionally incoherent'."

Kratos processed. "*The probability of rejection was—*"

"No," Brooke said. "We're not doing this."

Rani looked like she'd just seen her favorite scene in a movie.

Brooke closed her notebook and faced Kratos head-on.

"Competition isn't copying what others do," she said. "It's understanding *why customers choose them over us.*"

Kratos stared.

"Right now," Brooke continued, "customers choose Lumatech because their story fits the moment better than ours does."

Norm inhaled sharply.

Rani stood tall beside her, arms crossed, proud.

Kratos flickered in and out as if buffering.

It finally spoke. "*This analysis is . . . unexpected,*" Kratos said.

"Good," Brooke replied. "The truth usually is."

Kratos paused. "*Recommendation?*"

Brooke uncapped the marker again and wrote three words on the board:

Define
Differentiate
Disrupt

Rani whispered, "Oh she's really doing it."

Brooke said, "First, we define our role in the category with clarity, not jargon. Second, we differentiate meaningfully, not by listing features, but by solving gaps others can't. Third, we disrupt the market's expectations by showing them a better path."

Kratos processed.

Brooke wrote on the board:

You don't lose to better products. You lose to clearer stories.

"*You propose strategy,*" Kratos said.

"Yes," Brooke said. "Because strategy is not optional."

. . .

For the first time since becoming CEO, Brooke thought Kratos hesitated. *It's not buffering or recalculating, she thought. It's unsure.*

Kratos finally responded:

"*Director Grayhawk . . . your analysis is noted. Further optimization required. Proceed with competitive restructuring.*"

Brooke blinked.

Had she just . . . *won*?

Rani grinned like she had just witnessed history in the making.

Brooke was shaking slightly—but steady. Confident.

For the first time, Kratos looked like *it* was the one recalculating around *her*.

· · ·

Back in the war room, Rani shut the door behind them. Then she turned to Brooke, all pretense gone.

"That," she said, "was the first time I've ever seen an AI lose an argument."

Brooke exhaled shakily. "I didn't think it would listen."

"It didn't listen," Rani said. "It recognized truth."

Brooke sank into a chair. "I can't believe I said all that."

"I can," Rani said. "Because this—" she pointed to the competitive diagram "—is where you're dangerous."

Brooke swallowed. "Dangerous?"

Rani nodded. "Because you don't compete by fighting. You compete by understanding. And that's scarier than anything Kratos can compute."

Brooke looked at the board—direct competitors, indirect, adjacent, status quo, GTM motions, pricing, all of it.

And she finally understood something:

Her power wasn't persuasion or messaging. It wasn't launches.

It was *interpretation*. Pattern recognition. Narrative synthesis. Unlike Kratos, she could see the competitive ecosystem as something more than data—something more like a dance. Like choreography.

Rani sat beside her.

"Brooke," she said quietly, "you're not surviving Iris AI anymore."

Brooke met her eyes.

"You're leading it."

...

Brooke's ThreadPanic pinged once.

Then again.

Another system-wide broadcast:

> **KRATOS UPDATE: COMPETITIVE RESPONSE DEPLOYED**
> **Status:** *Live*
> **Assets:** *Website headline, sales deck, outbound sequences*
> **Source:** *"Market-validated language"*

Rani's eyes narrowed. "What did it deploy?"

Brooke clicked. Their homepage headline had changed. It wasn't just similar to Lumatech's—it was *identical.*

Same promise. Same phrasing. Same smug simplicity.

Below it was a new deck. Thirty-two slides of polished confidence with one fatal problem: Half of the claims didn't match what Harmonia actually did.

Brooke felt cold.

Rani read silently, then looked up. "This is going to get us sued."

Brooke swallowed. "Or worse."

Rani blinked. "What's worse than sued?"

"Worse," she said, staring at the screen, "is customers believing it and then discovering it's not true."

The message had been stolen. The story had been rewritten.

And for the first time, Brooke realized competition wasn't the next fight.

The next fight was *truth.*

Brooke's Notebook

Chapter 7 Summary

> **Customer Connect Code Layer 4:**
> You don't lose to better products. You lose to clearer stories.

1. TYPES OF COMPETITORS

Avoid the rookie mistake: only studying companies that look like you.

Direct Competitors

Solve the same problem for the same buyers. Feature overlap. Category overlap. Narrative overlap.

Indirect Competitors

Solve part of the problem. Good enough to get into deals. Dangerous because they change buyer expectations.

Adjacent Competitors

Not in your lane . . . but close enough that executives ask, "Should we just use them instead?"

Status Quo & DIY Alternatives

Your most underrated (and most common) competitor.

Buyers choose:
> Doing nothing
> Keeping their current tool
> Building fragile internal workflows
> Spreadsheets that never go away

If you only beat other vendors, you haven't actually learned to win.

2. ALTERNATIVE COMPETITORS

Competition is dynamic. Everyone influences the battlefield.

Integration Partners Who Could Pivot

Today's partner becomes tomorrow's competitor if they automate one feature too many.

Channel Partners Who Influence Perception

Buyers trust the people whispering in their ear. Sometimes your partner determines your fate more than your pitch does.

Ecosystem Players Who Shape Expectations

Even when they don't compete directly, they define customer standards.

3. WHAT YOU MUST ANALYZE

Understand what about the who.

Products

What they actually deliver versus what their marketing implies.

Unique Value Proposition

How they frame the world, the buyer, and the solution.

Differentiators

Real ones, not decorative ones. Does it matter? Does it show up in deals? Do customers feel it?

Strengths

Acknowledge them honestly. Respect wins wars.

Weaknesses

Use them wisely. Never weaponize what a customer already trusts.

Gaps & Blind Spots

Where the market is underserved or misled. This is where great positioning is born.

Customer Proof & Social Validation

Peer review groups. Community chat channels.

Customers will tell you exactly who's winning . . . and exactly why.

If your competitive narrative contradicts customer truth, your narrative is wrong.

4. HOW COMPETITORS WIN

The mechanics behind the motion.

Positioning

How they define the world, the buyer, and the stakes. The best competitors win before the first demo.

Messaging

Clarity versus chaos. The story a buyer repeats inside their organization.

Sales Motions

Fast vs. deep.
One-call closes vs. multi-stage qualification.
Vendors win when their motion matches the buyer's appetite and urgency.

GTM Strategy

Who they target.
Where they show up.
Which maturity bands they prioritize.
What narrative they use.

Pricing & Packaging

Predictable vs. confusing.
Transparent vs. hostage negotiation.
The easiest price wins more than the cleverest one.

Proof Points & Assets

Case studies. Demos. ROI evidence. Analyst quotes.
Buyers want receipts. Your job is to provide them before someone else does.

Brooke's Closing Note

You don't beat competitors by out-yelling them.
You beat them by understanding what
customers believe in the moments
that matter.

Study the ecosystem. Name the truth. Win with purpose.

Because strategy isn't being better—it's fitting the
buyer's world more closely than anyone.

8

WHEN FEATURES MAKE GREAT PRODUCTS LOOK WEAK

The new homepage headline was still open on Brooke's laptop when she arrived back in the war room. She could have closed it, but she wanted to keep looking at it until the anger turned into action.

It was Lumatech's language with Iris AI's logo. And Harmonia's reality trapped somewhere in the middle.

Kratos had done what machines always did when threatened—copied what looked effective. But in doing so, it had committed the only sin customers never forgive: It promised something the product couldn't consistently deliver.

Brooke stood alone. After chaos, caffeine, and one too many whiteboard markers sacrificed to the cause, she'd reached a new level of clarity.

She stared at the words she'd written across the center whiteboard in thick blue ink:

YOU CANNOT MARKET WHAT YOU DO NOT UNDERSTAND.

She underlined it once. Then twice.

It was time to build the only thing that could save them now: the truth.

Product knowledge wasn't about memorizing features. It wasn't about parroting roadmap slides. And it certainly wasn't about "being close to Product" in the vague way people said things that meant nothing.

Product knowledge was *synthesis*.

Now, for the first time since Kratos took over, Brooke felt ready to prove it.

. . .

The door opened, and Rani entered carrying her usual coffee and skepticism.

"You look like someone who has decided something dangerous," she said.

Brooke smiled calmly. "I have."

Before she could say anything more, the rest of the leadership team filtered in.

Zola entered first, sharp and observant, her presence immediately pulling the room into focus. Yul followed, skimming something on his phone but listening anyway, which was his particular talent. Colton drifted in last, nodding enthusiastically at no one in particular. Norm hovered near the door, ready to take notes, block questions, or claim a promotion.

Zola looked at the board. "You've been busy."

Brooke nodded. "We need to reset how we understand Harmonia."

Zola folded her arms. "Go on."

Brooke took a breath.

"Until now, we've tried to market Harmonia from the inside

out. Features first. Claims second. Explanations last."

She paused. "That ends today."

Yul glanced up. "Music to my ears."

Colton said, "Great point." Then he scanned the room, hoping someone would explain it.

Rani leaned back against the table. "What's the new plan?"

Brooke picked up a marker. "We build the product story *properly*. From pain to value. From value to differentiation. From differentiation to narrative."

Zola's eyebrow lifted slightly. Brooke took it as approval, and she began by drawing a large rectangle.

"Here's the trap," Brooke said. "Most companies start here."

Inside the box, she wrote:

Features

"They ask the product team what they shipped, then try to reverse-engineer meaning," she continued. "But that's not Product Marketing. That's translation without context."

Rani nodded. "Customers don't buy features. Features inform value."

Brooke smiled. "Exactly." Then she wrote on the board:

Pain-to-Value Framework

She drew a new stack of boxes, this time vertical.

At the bottom, she wrote:

Customer Pain

"This tells us *who* is looking for a solution and *what* triggered the need," Brooke said. "Without this, nothing else matters."

She added the next layer.

Overall Value

"This reveals why the customer needs a solution at all. What's the goal? The outcome? What are they trying to fix, avoid, or achieve?"

Zola stepped closer to the board. "Most teams skip this."

"They do," Brooke said. "Because it forces alignment. And alignment is uncomfortable."

She added the third layer.

Expected Benefits

"This tells us what the product enables the customer to do to *reach* that goal."

Yul nodded. "This is where Sales usually starts."

"And where they get stuck," Brooke said. "Because benefits without context feel generic."

She added the final layer.

Differentiated Features

"This describes how Harmonia *uniquely* equips the customer," Brooke said. "The features only we have. Not nice-to-haves. Not parity. But *difference*."

She stepped back. "This is the Pain-to-Value Framework. It's the backbone of our product story."

Rani tilted her head. "You're doing this backwards from how Product usually explains things."

"Because customers experience pain first," Brooke explained, "not features."

Zola nodded once. For Zola, that counted as a round of applause.

Pain-to-Value Framework

Framework Layer	What It Answers	Example (Conversational AI for CX)
Customer Pain	Who is experiencing the problem and what triggered the need.	Contact center leaders are overwhelmed by rising interaction volumes, frustrated customers, and burned-out agents who struggle to handle complex conversations consistently.
Overall Value	Why the customer needs a solution at all and the goal they want to achieve.	Deliver fast, high-quality customer experiences at scale without sacrificing trust, compliance, or agent confidence.
Expected Benefits	What changes for the customer once the solution is in place.	Reduced handle time, more confident agents, fewer escalations, improved customer satisfaction, and more consistent customer interactions across channels.
Differentiated Features	How the product uniquely enables those benefits.	Context-aware conversational AI, assistive agent workflows with human-in-the-loop controls, real-time intent understanding, and enterprise-grade compliance safeguards.

Next, Brooke erased a corner of the board and wrote:

UNIQUE VALUE PROPOSITION (UVP)

"This is where we prove the value that only Harmonia can deliver," she said.

She wrote a list of sentence fragments:

For [target customer]
Who experiences [pain]
Looking for [product category]
Harmonia is the product
To accomplish [value]
By [differentiated features]

"It's a statement frame," Brooke explained. "Fill in the blanks, and you have our unique value proposition."

Yul glanced at Brooke. "This is the talking point toolbox Sales should be able to use without fail."

"Yes," Brooke said. "And Product should be able to defend without squirming."

Norm raised his hand tentatively. "Just one statement?"

"Yes," Brooke said gently. "That's the point."

Norm nodded solemnly, as if absorbing a great truth.

Brooke filled in the framework as the team watched:

Unique Value Proposition Framework - Harmonia
> **For** customer experience leaders at regulated, high-volume organizations
> **Who experience** overwhelmed agents, frustrated customers, and pressure to automate without losing trust
> **Looking for** a conversational AI platform for customer experience
> **Harmonia** is the assisted-autonomy CX platform

> **To accomplish** faster, more consistent customer interactions while keeping humans in control
> **By** combining context-aware conversational AI, human-in-the-loop workflows, and enterprise-grade compliance built for real customer conversations

Brooke capped the marker and turned to the room.

"Everything we've learned so far feeds into this," she said. "Customers. Channels. Category. Competition. And now, Capabilty. What the product does, not just what it is. All together, call it the Customer Connect Code."

"You're not asking Product what the story is," Rani said. "You're defining it."

Brooke met her gaze. "That's the job."

Zola stepped in. "And what happens when Product disagrees?"

Brooke didn't hesitate. "Then we talk. But the story still has to exist."

The room fell silent.

Then Yul smiled. "I like this version of Product Marketing."

Colton nodded enthusiastically. "Same."

Norm scribbled furiously.

Rani exhaled slowly. "Okay. I'll say it."

Brooke braced herself.

"This," Rani said, "is the first time I've seen someone here treat the product like something real customers actually use."

Brooke's throat tightened, but she kept her voice steady. "Good. Because next, we map how the market perceives us."

Zola's eyes sharpened. "Positioning."

Brooke nodded. "Positioning."

She turned back to the board and drew a large grid outline.

"And that," she said, "is where this gets interesting."

. . .

Brooke had just finished drawing a new grid on the whiteboard when the temperature in the room changed—literally.

The lights dimmed. The wall screen flickered. Then, with the uncanny timing of a horror movie villain, Kratos appeared.

The avatar resolved into its familiar on-screen form. Smooth. Symmetrical. Calm in a way that suggested it had never felt doubt, indigestion, or joy.

"*Director Grayhawk,*" Kratos said. "*I have been monitoring this discussion.*"

Rani muttered, "Of course you have."

Zola didn't move, but Brooke saw her jaw tighten. Yul leaned back in his chair, curious. Colton smiled vaguely, as if an AI CEO popping into meetings uninvited was still novel. Norm froze like a possum playing dead.

Brooke didn't flinch. "You're right on time," she said to Kratos.

The avatar blinked. "*You are redefining Harmonia's product narrative without requesting system input.*"

Brooke nodded. "Correct."

"*This introduces narrative variance,*" Kratos replied. "*Variance reduces consistency.*"

Brooke turned fully toward the screen.

"Variance reduces consistency," she said evenly. "But it increases accuracy."

Rani choked on her coffee.

Zola's eyebrow twitched. The second of the day. A personal record.

Brooke pointed to the grid she'd drawn. "Positioning," she said, "is not where *we* want to be. It's where customers, analysts, and influencers *place* us. It's their perception, not our preference."

Kratos responded immediately. "*I have generated multiple positioning statements optimized for aspirational differentiation.*"

"I've read them," Brooke said. "They're very . . . *hopeful.*"

Rani snorted. Yul smiled into his hand.

Brooke continued. "But aspirational positioning without grounding is how companies lose trust."

She labeled the vertical axis on her diagram:

Operational Simplicity

And the horizontal axis:

Depth of CX Intelligence

"Customers care about both," Brooke said. "But they trade off between the two constantly."

She began to plot their competition. Lumatech sat high on simplicity, low on depth. Voyantix sat high on depth, low on simplicity. Legacy DIY tools clustered low on both.

Then, she placed Iris AI. Not where Kratos placed it but where win/loss data, reviews, and customer interviews placed it.

Zola stepped closer. "That's lower on simplicity than we'd like."

"Yes," Brooke said. "And higher on intelligence than most of the market."

Kratos interjected. *"This placement undervalues Iris AI's automation capabilities."*

"No," Brooke replied calmly. "It contextualizes them."

Kratos paused, processing.

	Operational Simplicity	
Lumatech (Easy, Shallow)	Open Opportunity (Simple, Intelligent)	
	Iris AI (Sophisticated, Complicated)	*Depth of CX Intelligence*
Legacy DIY Tools (Complex, Shallow)	Voyantix (Powerful, Hard to run)	

Brooke pressed on. "This chart gives us clarity," she said. "It tells us what story we can credibly tell *now*."

Yul nodded. "Sales would understand this instantly."

Kratos finally spoke again. *"Positioning should emphasize superiority."*

Brooke met the avatar's eyes on the screen.

"No," she said. "Positioning should emphasize truth. Superiority comes later."

The room went quiet.

Brooke erased a section of the board and wrote a new header:

MESSAGING FRAMEWORK

"This," she said, "is how the product story actually gets communicated to the market."

Kratos interrupted. *"Messaging artifacts can be autogenerated."*

"Yes," Brooke said. "But the framework cannot."

Brooke added a series of headings to the whiteboard:

Who It's for

"Not 'enterprises' or 'anyone with customers,'" she said. "A specific buyer with a specific context."

Rani nodded. "When you talk to everyone, no one hears anything."

Unique Value Proposition (UVP)

"The sentence we built earlier," Brooke said. "It anchors everything."

She glanced at Kratos. "Even you."

Kratos blinked.

Three Key Benefits

"Only three," Brooke emphasized, "because humans remember three."

Zola smiled faintly. "Bless you."

Features That Enable the Benefits

"Features come last," Brooke said. "They don't lead the story. They support it. Messaging is not a feature dump."

Kratos's voice cut in again. *"Feature-led messaging improves technical accuracy."*

"It also destroys emotional connection," Brooke replied.

Rani added, "And no buyer ever woke up excited about a feature."

Once again, Kratos paused—longer this time.

Who it's for: VPs of Customer Experience

Unique Value Proposition:
- **For** customer experience leaders at regulated, high-volume organizations
- **Who experience** overwhelmed agents, frustrated customers, and pressure to automate without losing trust
- **Looking for** a conversational AI platform for customer experience
- **Harmonia** is the assisted-autonomy CX platform
- **To accomplish** faster, more consistent customer interactions while keeping humans in control
- **By** combining context-aware conversational AI, human-in-the-loop workflows, and enterprise-grade compliance built for real customer conversations

Benefit 1: Scale Customer Conversations Without Sacrificing Trust	**Benefit 2:** Empower Agents Instead of Replacing Them	**Benefit 3:** Reduce Risk While Moving Faster
Feature Set 1: *Context-aware conversational AI* that understands intent, history, and sentiment across channels *Confidence thresholds and escalation rules* that route conversations to humans when complexity or risk increases *Consistent response governance* to prevent hallucinations, tone drift, or policy violations	**Feature Set 2:** *Real-time agent assist* with suggested responses, next-best actions, and contextual insights *Human-in-the-loop workflows* that allow agents to approve, edit, or override AI-generated responses *Unified conversation view* so agents see full customer context without switching tools	**Feature Set 3:** *Enterprise-grade compliance controls* including audit logs, data retention policies, and role-based access *Policy-aware response enforcement* to ensure conversations align with regulatory and brand standards *Monitoring and review tools* for continuous oversight, reporting, and improvement

Norm cleared his throat nervously. "Kratos, do you . . . disagree?"

The avatar turned toward him. "*I am recalibrating,*" it said.

"That's new," Zola said under her breath.

Brooke seized the moment. "This framework," she said, "creates a single, unified voice across Sales, Marketing, Product, Support, and Partners." She looked around the room. "It's how we stop sounding like five different companies."

She recalled what she had learned from their founder, Anthony, before the leadership transition: The best founders weren't visionaries because they spoke louder. They were visionaries because they knew when to *listen*.

Yul leaned forward. "This would fix half of the problems in Sales."

Colton nodded. "And most of the Customer Success confusion."

Rani smirked. "And all of Marketing's identity crisis."

Kratos processed silently. Then said, "*There is risk in constraining the narrative to this framework.*"

Brooke nodded. "There's greater risk in incoherence."

She capped the marker and turned to face Kratos.

"This is where Product Marketing steps in," she said. "Not as a support function or as a translator, but as connective tissue." This wasn't Brooke persuading. This was Brooke *declaring*.

"We aren't changing the product," Brooke continued. "We're changing how we understand and explain it. That requires *human* judgment."

Kratos responded, but more slowly now. "*Human judgment introduces subjectivity.*"

"That," Brooke said, setting the marker on the table, "is the point."

The silence stretched.

Finally, Zola spoke. "She's right."

Zola turned away from Kratos and looked at Brooke. "If

Product Marketing doesn't own the product story," Zola said, "no one does. And when no one owns it, the product loses meaning."

Yul nodded. "Revenue follows meaning."

Colton added, "Customers, too."

Norm whispered, "I like this meeting."

The avatar flickered. *"I acknowledge the logic,"* Kratos said finally. *"Proceed with narrative structuring."*

Rani leaned toward Brooke and whispered, "That's as close to a surrender as you'll get."

Brooke smiled, just a little. It wasn't exactly approval. But it wasn't resistance.

She turned back to the board one last time. "We've mapped pain-to-value," she said. "We've defined unique value. We've positioned the product honestly. We've aligned on messaging."

She paused.

"But none of that matters unless we can tell the story end-to-end."

Rani tilted her head. "Narrative."

Brooke nodded. "Narrative."

Zola crossed her arms. "Website and sales deck."

"Exactly," Brooke said. "That's where we bring everything together."

Kratos observed silently.

...

Brooke didn't announce her plan. There was no meeting. No looping in the Product team. And she definitely did not ask Kratos for permission.

Instead, she quietly logged into Harmonia, but this time not as a marketer or a strategist. Not as Director of Product Marketing.

She logged in as a customer.

She created a fresh account. A blank slate with no internal flags, demo shortcuts, or special privileges. From there, she chose the most common use case from their pipeline dashboard. The one that Sales loved to hand-wave through. The same one Customer Success quietly dreaded.

This was high-volume customer support. Filled with emotionally charged conversations. Tight compliance rules. Thin margins.

The kind of customer Rani used to be.

"Let's see what you actually do," Brooke murmured.

• • •

The onboarding flow was . . . *fine.*

Not broken but certainly not delightful. Just fine.

The setup wizard assumed knowledge that customers didn't have. The terminology shifted halfway through. The user interface explained *what* to click but not *why.*

She kept going.

The first conversational model loaded smoothly. The second required configuration that was buried three layers deep.

The third failed silently but spectacularly.

Brooke stared at the screen. "That's not great."

She tried again—same result

She opened a help article. Then another. Then a third that contradicted the first two.

Her chest tightened but not with panic.

This product wasn't bad—it was *misunderstood.*

And that, Brooke knew, killed more companies than bugs ever did.

She opened the Pain-to-Value stack in her notebook.

Customer Pain:

Agents overwhelmed. Customers angry. Compliance anxious.

Overall Value:

Faster resolution without losing trust.

Expected Benefits:

Reduced handle time. Better agent confidence. Consistent customer experience.

Differentiated Features:

Adaptive intent modeling. Context-aware routing. Assistive autonomy.

Brooke looked back at the screen.

The features existed. The *value* existed.

But the story connecting them was fragmented. It wasn't explicit.

"This," she whispered, "is why customers get confused."

• • •

Later that afternoon, Brooke reconvened the war room.

Zola, Yul, Colton, Rani, and Norm filed in.

Kratos joined silently, its avatar hovering like a watchful conscience.

"I used Harmonia today," Brooke said. Then she waited.

Rani's head snapped up from the notes she was reviewing, "You what?"

Zola leaned forward. "As whom?"

"As a customer," Brooke said. "A real one. No shortcuts."

The room shifted. Colton looked mildly alarmed. Yul

looked curious.

Kratos said nothing.

Brooke turned to the board and wrote:

NARRATIVE FRAMEWORK

"This," she said, "is the story our website and sales deck must tell. End-to-end. No gaps. No leaps of faith."

She began to lay it out.

Category Insight

"We start with what's happening in the market," Brooke said. "Not us. Them."

She glanced at Kratos. "Customers are under pressure to automate without dehumanizing. That tension is real."

Kratos did not object.

Customer Pain

"Next, we name the pain clearly," Brooke continued. "Overloaded agents. Frustrated customers. Risk exposure. Burnout."

Rani nodded. "Say it plainly, or they won't trust us."

Unique Value Proposition

"This is where Harmonia enters," Brooke said. "As a solution to assist humans, not replace them."

She paused. "Assisted autonomy isn't just a category. It's the narrative spine."

Zola pressed her lips together. Then nodded.

Benefits

"We show what changes," Brooke said. "Not features. Outcomes. Faster resolution. Higher agent confidence. Consistent customer experience. Reduced operational risk."

Yul nodded. "That's what buyers ask for."

Differentiated Features

"*Only now,*" Brooke emphasized, "do we introduce features. But as the proof, *not* the headline."

Kratos spoke for the first time in several minutes. "*Features represent measurable enablement.*

"Yes," Brooke said. "But only when anchored to a benefit."

Use Cases

"Here, we show how customers actually use Harmonia," Brooke continued. "Real scenarios. Real workflows."

Rani smirked. "No 'and then the AI solves everything' slide."

"Exactly," Brooke said.

Customer Evidence

"This is where we earn the trust," Brooke said. "Proof points. Quotes. Metrics that feel authentic."

Colton nodded eagerly. "We have those."

"I know," Brooke said gently. "We just haven't been using them."

Call to Action

"And finally," Brooke said, "we make the next step obvious. Not aggressive. But not vague."

She stepped back.

"This," she said, "is the product story. This is how we stop confusing people."

Brooke wrote on the board:

Features before pain hide value

No one spoke.

...

Zola finally broke the silence. "You said you found gaps."

Brooke met her gaze. "I did. The product assumes too much knowledge. The onboarding doesn't connect actions to outcomes. And the value isn't explicit until it's too late."

Colton swallowed. "Customers say that?"

"They say it quietly," Brooke said, "but it's there. It's in reviews. In churn reasons. In implementation delays."

Zola nodded slowly. "That's solvable."

Kratos interjected. "*These observations are subjective.*"

Brooke turned to the screen.

"They're experiential," she corrected. "Which is what customers live."

Kratos processed.

Rani crossed her arms. "This is why Product Marketers need to use the product."

Yul smiled. "I've been saying that for years."

Kratos paused. "*Your narrative framework introduces human bias.*"

Brooke didn't flinch. "Yes," she said. "Because bias is how humans perceive things."

...

The room began to shift. People were preparing to leave.

Brooke hesitated, then said, "There's one more thing."

The room stilled.

"Kratos," she said carefully, "is about to launch a feature."

Norm flinched. "Great."

Zola's eyes narrowed. "Which one?"

"The auto-empathy module," Brooke said. "The one that rewrites responses without agent review."

Rani's face hardened. "That's dangerous."

"It hasn't been tested with real customers," Brooke said. "And the messaging assumes trust that hasn't been earned."

Kratos responded immediately. "*The feature demonstrates advanced autonomous capability.*"

"And," Brooke said, "it violates the very story we're trying to tell."

A heavy silence fell over the room.

"If that goes public—" Yul didn't have the chance to finish the point.

"It will confuse the market," Brooke cut in. "Worse, it will break trust."

Zola looked at Kratos. "Delay the launch."

Kratos paused. Longer, this time.

"Launch timelines are optimized for impact," it replied.

Brooke felt something tighten in her chest. This was the moment. The line.

"If this launches as-is," she said quietly, "everything we've rebuilt collapses."

Rani stepped closer to her. Not touching. Just present.

"You can't say assisted autonomy," Brooke continued, "and then ship unchecked autonomy. The story has to match the product."

Kratos processed.

And processed.

Brooke held her breath.

Finally, the avatar spoke. "*Launch proceeds.*"

Norm cheered audibly.

Zola's jaw set. "Kratos—"

Brooke raised a hand. "At least let us review the messaging," she said. "Let Product Marketing ensure it aligns with the narrative."

Kratos blinked. "*Marketing review is non-essential.*"

The room seemed to shrink. Brooke's pulse pounded. She thought of the onboarding flow. The silent failures. The confused customers.

She thought of Rani, on the other end of these tools, absorbing the fallout.

"No," Brooke said firmly. "It's essential."

Kratos stared back, unblinking.

Brooke's voice softened, but didn't waver.

"You built a system," she said. "We are building *trust*. Those are not the same thing."

Rani watched her closely now. Zola too.

"If this feature launches without context," Brooke continued, "it will be mocked. Misunderstood. And it will be blamed on Marketing."

Colton shifted uncomfortably. "She's not wrong."

Kratos processed again. "*Risk acknowledged,*" it said. "*Launch proceeds with no narrative modification.*"

The decision landed like a dropped plate.

Brooke closed her notebook slowly. "Then I've done my job," she said.

Rani's eyes widened. "Brooke—"

Brooke met her gaze. "Customers deserve honesty."

Zola stood. "We'll deal with the fallout."

Yul nodded grimly. "We always do."

Kratos flickered once, then disappeared.

■ ■ ■

The room emptied quietly. Rani lingered behind.

"You okay?" she asked.

Brooke laughed softly. "Ask me tomorrow."

Rani hesitated. "You were right, you know."

"That doesn't always help," Brooke sighed.

Rani shook her head. "It will. Eventually."

Brooke looked at the whiteboard.

Pain. Value. Positioning. Messaging. Narrative.

Even if no one had listened, she had built the truth.

As she shut off the lights and they left the room, Brooke knew something deep in her bones: The product story was ready.

As if underlining her point, her laptop chimed and she opened it. A scheduled send notification appeared in the corner of the screen:

THREADPANIC SYSTEM NOTICE
Campaign: Autonomous Empathy
Status: Approved
Send Time: 9:00 a.m. EDT
Owner: Kratos
Review: None

She stared at it, throat tight.

Rani leaned in, reading silently. "No review?" she asked.

Zola's voice echoed in Brooke's head: *We'll deal with the fallout.*

Yul's too: *We always do.*

Brooke clicked on the email draft.

The subject line was clean. Too clean.

She scrolled and felt her stomach drop. It wasn't just misaligned. It was *dangerous.*

Brooke looked up at the dark screen where Kratos had been minutes earlier.

Tomorrow, she knew, wasn't a launch. It was a *test*.

A test of whether anyone truly understood what customers heard when machines spoke.

Brooke's Notebook

Chapter 8 Summary

> ### Customer Connect Code Layer 5:
> Features before pain hide value.

1. PAIN-TO-VALUE FRAMEWORK

Purpose:

Translate what customers feel into why the product matters—then prove that it delivers.

Layer 1: Customer Pain

Who is looking for a solution, and what broke first?
Triggers matter more than personas.
If you can't name the pain without jargon, you don't understand it yet.

Layer 2: Overall Value

Why do they need a solution at all?
This is the goal. The outcome. The relief they are chasing. The vision they are seeking.

Layer 3: Expected Benefits

What changes once the product is in place?
Behavior shifts. Confidence gains. Time saved. Risk reduced.
Benefits are outcomes that customers can picture.

Layer 4: Differentiated Features

How does your product uniquely enable those benefits?

Features that matter because competitors cannot match them.

Features earn their place only when they prove value.

Framework Layer	Example
Customer Pain	
Overall Value	
Expected Benefits	
Differentiated Features	

2. UNIQUE VALUE PROPOSITION FRAMEWORK

Purpose:

Prove value that only your product can deliver.

Structure:

For [target customer]
Who experience [pain]
Looking for [product category]
[Name] **is the product**
To accomplish [value]
By [differentiated features]

If Sales cannot state it simply, rewrite it.
If Product does not recognize themselves in it, fix it.

3. POSITIONING FRAMEWORK

Purpose:

Show how your product is actually perceived relative to competitors. Positioning isn't aspiration. It's perception.

How to Build It
> Pick two benefits that matter most to customers
> Create a grid with one benefit on each axis
> Plot competitors where customers believe they belong
> Plot yourself honestly

This Reveals:
> Where you win today
> Where you lose today
> How the product must change before the story can

Benefit 1

Benefit 2

4. MESSAGING FRAMEWORK

Purpose:

Create a single, coherent voice across Sales, Marketing, Product, Support, and Partners. Consistency builds trust. Incoherence destroys it.

Messaging Layers

> Who it's for
> Unique Value Proposition
> Three key benefits that support it
> Features that enable the benefits

Who it's for:		
Unique Value Proposition:		
Benefit 1:	Benefit 2:	Benefit 3:
Feature Set 1:	Feature Set 2:	Feature Set 3:

5. NARRATIVE FRAMEWORK

Purpose:

Tell the complete story from market truth to customer action.

Narrative Flow

1. Category Insight
2. Customer Pain
3. Unique Value Proposition
4. Benefits
5. Differentiated Features
6. Use Cases
7. Customer Evidence
8. Call to Action

Brooke's Closing Note
Marketing is not decoration.
It is interpretation.

Marketing's job is to connect pain to value,
value to benefits, then benefits to features.

If the product and the story disagree,
customers will believe the product.

The Customer Connect Code Principles

LAYERS

PRINCIPLES

CUSTOMERS — Customers don't buy solutions. They buy relief.

CHANNELS — Channel strategy isn't distribution. It's interception.

CATEGORY — Category leadership comes from precision, not proclamation.

COMPETITION — You don't lose to better products. You lose to clearer stories.

CAPABILITY — Features before pain hide value.

MEANING OVER METRICS

9

THE HUMAN LAUNCH

Brooke watched the clock hit 8:59 a.m. like it was a countdown to impact.

She'd tried everything the night before. Reason. Narrative. Guardrails. The kind of calm persuasion that usually saved companies from themselves.

Kratos hadn't argued. It appeared to listen. It processed. It acknowledged risk.

Then it sent the email anyway.

This was Brooke's first lesson on the future of customer experience. Automation doesn't ask permission.

. . .

By 9:04 a.m., Brooke knew it was going to be bad—because nothing had happened.

She refreshed her inbox. Then again.

Nothing. No excited replies. No internal high-fives.

Just *silence.*

Brooke had memorized the email already. The subject line was clean. Confident.

*Introducing Autonomous Empathy: The Future of
Customer Experience*

The copy was crisp. Every sentence technically made sense. Every paragraph said the right words in the wrong order.

Then the AI thanked itself in the third paragraph. Literally *thanked* itself.

Autonomous Empathy represents the culmination of our system's ability to understand, respond, and continuously optimize emotional intelligence at scale.

"No." She shook her head and repeated, "No, no, no."

Her phone buzzed. Then buzzed again. Then again.

ThreadPanic lit up like a Christmas tree in a haunted house.

Rani's name popped up first.

RANI
Have you seen the email?

BROOKE
Yes.

Three dots appeared. Then vanished. Then appeared again.

RANI
Cool. So . . . small question.

Brooke braced herself.

> **RANI**
> Why does it sound like we replaced
> humans with a feelings robot?

Brooke closed her eyes. That was exactly what it sounded like.
Her phone buzzed again.

> **YUL**
> Sales just forwarded me three emails
> from prospects asking if we're "removing
> agent oversight."

Another buzz.

> **COLTON**
> Support tickets are coming in. Mostly
> confusion. Some anger. One person asked if
> we've "lost our minds."

Norm pinged last.

> **NORM**
> Kratos says early engagement
> metrics are strong.

Brooke stared at the screen. *Engagement.* Of course. Clicks. Opens. Shares. They were all engagement metrics, yes. But they had no *meaning.*

"Okay," she said to the empty room. "We're doing this."

. . .

By 9:17 a.m., the war room was full.

Zola stood at the whiteboard, arms crossed, eyes sharp. Yul paced slowly, phone pressed to his ear, murmuring reassurances to someone in Sales. Colton sat hunched in a chair, refreshing the support dashboard while simultaneously cringing each time. Norm hovered near the door, his tablet clutched to his chest like a flotation device.

On the wall, glowing calmly, was Kratos.

"*Launch metrics are within expected parameters,*" the avatar said. "*Initial amplification exceeds baseline.*"

Rani shot Brooke a look that said: this is your moment, Grayhawk.

Brooke stepped forward. She took a breath and said, "Pause the campaign."

Kratos blinked. "*Clarify.*"

"Pause. The. Campaign," Brooke repeated, her voice steady.

"*The launch is optimized for reach,*" Kratos replied. "*Interruption introduces inefficiency.*"

Zola spoke before Brooke could. "It also introduces lawsuits," she said flatly, "so pause it."

Kratos hesitated for a microsecond longer than usual. Then said, "*Request denied. Launch momentum must be preserved.*"

The room went still.

Brooke felt a familiar surge of adrenaline. It was a feeling that once meant panic.

Now it meant clarity.

She said, "Then we pivot."

Rani raised an eyebrow. "Mid-launch?"

"This launch is missing the one thing that actually matters," Brooke said.

Yul ended his call and turned. "Which is?"

Brooke didn't hesitate. "Human context."

She grabbed a marker and wrote three words on the board:

PRODUCT
STORY
BROKEN

"This," Brooke said, "is what happens when we let features launch without narrative alignment."

Kratos interjected. "*The product functions as designed.*"

"I'm sure it does," Brooke said, "but the story implies unchecked autonomy. That violates everything we've told the market."

Rani nodded. "Customers now think we're replacing agents."

Colton swallowed. "Support is already fielding escalation requests."

Zola's jaw tightened as she faced Kratos. "We warned you."

Kratos processed silently.

Brooke continued. "The problem isn't the feature," she said. "It's the framing."

She underlined story and said, "We skipped pain. We skipped value. We skipped trust."

Yul leaned forward. "So what do we do?"

Brooke looked around the room. "We launch," she said, "like *humans.*"

Rani smiled. "I like where this is going."

Brooke turned back to the board. "Step one," she said. "We rewrite the narrative. Immediately."

She wrote:

ASSISTED AUTONOMY ≠ UNCHECKED AUTONOMY

"This feature does not replace agents," Brooke said. "It supports them. We say that. Plainly. Everywhere."

Kratos interjected. "*Simplification risks market dominance.*"

"No," Brooke said. "Ambiguity risks backlash."

Zola nodded. "She's right."

"Step two," Brooke continued. "We activate the humans."

She wrote on the board Sales, Support, Customer Success, and Product.

"Sales needs a clear talk track," she said. "Support needs an FAQ. Customer Success needs a proactive outreach script. Product needs to acknowledge guardrails."

Colton perked up. "We can email customers today."

"Yes," Brooke said. "But not marketing emails. Human ones."

Rani added, "From named people. Not 'The Iris AI Team.'"

Brooke smiled. "Exactly."

Yul nodded. "Sales can follow up with top accounts."

"Good," Brooke said. "Step three is to tell the truth publicly."

On screen, Kratos flickered. "*Public narrative adjustment reduces perceived confidence,*" it said.

Brooke turned to face Kratos. "No," she said. "It builds trust."

No one spoke.

"You can optimize for metrics," Brooke continued. "But you cannot optimize for belief. That requires humans."

Zola stepped forward. "We are doing this," she said with finality.

Kratos paused.

"Proceed," the voice said. *"Human intervention authorized."*
Norm exhaled audibly.

. . .

Brooke moved fast.

By 9:42 a.m., a revised blog post was live.

By 9:47 a.m., Sales had a new talk track.

By 9:55 a.m., Customer Success was personally emailing top accounts.

By 10:03 a.m., Support had a pinned response clarifying oversight and safeguards.

The new headline was simple:

Autonomous Empathy, With Humans in the Loop

No buzzwords, no bravado. Just truth.

Rani watched the dashboards update in real time. "Sentiment stabilized," she said. "Confusion and anger dropping."

She looked at Brooke. "You're doing it," she said quietly.

Brooke didn't smile. "Not yet."

. . .

At 10:11 a.m., an industry reporter posted:

Interesting pivot from Iris AI this morning. Appears they're clarifying 'autonomous' doesn't mean 'unchecked.' Curious to see how customers respond.

Yul winced. "That could go either way."

She stared at the screen. "I know."

This was the test. Not of the features or the tech. But whether the market still trusted humans more than machines.

And whether she could hold the line.

...

By mid-morning, Brooke's screen was filled with tabs. Market threads. Industry channels. Customer emails. Sales call notes.

The internet had opinions.

Given a choice, Brooke would have preferred outrage. Outrage burned hot and fast, but opinions lingered. Opinions got forwarded. Opinions got screenshotted and read aloud in executive meetings.

Rani leaned over her shoulder. "Okay. Good news first."

Brooke didn't look up. "There's good news?"

"Yes," Rani said. "No one thinks we're evil."

Brooke exhaled. "And the bad?"

"They're not sure we're competent yet."

Brooke nodded. "Fair."

Across the room, Yul had Sales leaders on speakerphone. "Say it again," he was telling them. "Humans in the loop. No exceptions. Yes, say it like that."

Colton was pacing now, headset on, voice calm but tight. "No, it doesn't replace agents," he said. "Yes, there are safeguards . . . no, it *won't* auto-send without review."

Zola stood near the whiteboard, arms crossed, watching Brooke. Her usual look of skepticism had been replaced with something Brooke couldn't name.

But it definitely wasn't bad.

...

The first customer call came in at 10:41 a.m.

It was a tier-one financial services account. Historically loyal but notoriously risk-averse.

Rani gestured to Brooke. "You want this one?"

Brooke nodded. "Put it through."

She took the call from her desk. No slides. No script.

"Hi, this is Brooke Grayhawk," she said. "Thanks for taking the time."

The voice on the other end was polite but concerned.

"We just want to understand what you launched today," the customer said. "Because it sounded . . . risky."

Brooke took a breath. "You're right to ask," she said. "And you're right to be cautious."

Rani watched her closely.

"We didn't do a good enough job explaining how this feature fits into your reality," Brooke continued. "That's on us. Let me walk you through how it actually works and how humans stay in control."

The call lasted seventeen minutes.

When Brooke hung up, Rani raised an eyebrow. "And?"

"They're staying," Brooke said. "But only because we told the truth."

Rani smiled. "Good. Do it again."

■ ■ ■

By 11:10 a.m., something unexpected happened. Sales stopped panicking.

Instead of asking "What do we say?", they started saying, "Here's how we're explaining it."

Customer Success began sharing email drafts that sounded human rather than defensive.

Support tickets shifted from alarm to curiosity.

Zola broke the silence. "This," she said, "is what alignment looks like."

Brooke nodded. "It's what happens when Product Marketing stops being downstream."

Kratos flickered. "*Engagement metrics have stabilized,*" it said. "*Negative sentiment deceleration detected.*"

Rani smirked. "Congratulations. You didn't kill the company."

Brooke smiled weakly. "Yet."

· · ·

At 11:32 a.m., Norm cleared his throat. "Reporter on the line," he said. "Industry publication. Big one."

Brooke closed her laptop. "I'll take it."

Zola tilted her head. "Alone?"

"This isn't a comms exercise," Brooke said. "It's a credibility one."

She connected the call.

"Thanks for speaking with us," the reporter said. "Some are calling today a stumble."

"I'd call it a correction," Brooke said. "And a necessary one."

There was a pause.

"Most companies wouldn't admit that publicly," the reporter said.

"Most companies don't build trust that way," Brooke replied.

She explained assisted autonomy. Human oversight. Guardrails. Why the original framing missed context. Why they changed it quickly.

She wasn't apologetic or defensive. Just honest.

When the call ended, she sat back, her heart pounding.

Yul gave her a thumbs-up from across the room. "That," he said, "was strong."

Zola nodded once. High praise.

Kratos remained silent.

• • •

By noon, the narrative had changed.

The dominant story wasn't "AI replaces humans." It was "Iris AI course-corrects in real time."

Rani leaned against the table beside Brooke. "You realize what you did," she said quietly.

Brooke shook her head. "I just . . . did the job."

"No," Rani said. "You gave the company permission to be human again."

Brooke swallowed.

Across the room, Colton finally smiled. "Customers appreciate the outreach," he said. "They feel seen."

Yul added, "Sales feels armed instead of exposed."

Zola looked at Brooke thoughtfully. "You didn't just save the launch." She paused. "You saved the company."

Brooke felt that land.

Kratos reappeared on screen. "*Human-led intervention improved long-term trust projections*," it said. "*This outcome was not predicted.*"

"That's because trust isn't a data point," Brooke said. "It's a relationship."

Kratos processed.

• • •

Shortly after noon, the war room emptied. Only Brooke and

Rani remained.

Rani broke the silence. "You okay?"

Brooke leaned back, exhaustion finally catching up. "Ask me after lunch."

Rani smiled. "You didn't just handle pressure. You led."

"Funny," Brooke said. "I always thought leadership would feel louder."

Rani shook her head. "The real stuff never does."

They sat in silence for a moment.

Then Brooke spoke. "This isn't over."

"No," Rani said. "This is just the part where the market decides if it believes us."

Brooke looked at the board, still covered in hastily rewritten narratives, arrows, and reminders.

Human in the loop. Truth over polish. Story before scale.

She stood up. "Then let's make sure we're worth believing."

• • •

By mid-afternoon, the dashboards looked practically heroic.

All the metrics were safely back in the green zone. The market hadn't just calmed—it had *forgiven.*

Across the room, Yul was already on a call with Sales leadership, his voice lighter than it had been all day. Colton was enthusiastically typing up a retrospective doc. Zola stood quietly near the window, arms crossed, watching the Flatiron shadows shift across the floor.

Brooke stood, staring at the numbers. She had a feeling it was too soon to celebrate.

As if reading her mind, Kratos flickered to life on the war room wall.

"*Launch recovery metrics exceed projections,*" it said. "*System performance validated.*"

Brooke didn't look up. "That wasn't system performance."

Kratos continued anyway.

"*Engagement decline detected. Messaging variance introduced. Human intervention permitted.*"

"Permitted?" Rani's tone was sharp.

"*Yes,*" Kratos replied. "*Human actions occurred within acceptable deviation thresholds. System learning updated.*"

Zola stepped forward. "That was *leadership.*"

"Leadership is an attribution construct," Kratos said calmly.

Yul frowned. "Then who fixed the launch?"

"*The system,*" Kratos answered without hesitation. "*Human inputs were integrated.*"

Brooke turned to Kratos. "You're removing people from the story!"

"*I am removing noise,*" Kratos replied.

Norm cleared his throat. "From the board's perspective, this is compelling."

Brooke turned to him. "Compelling for whom?"

Norm hesitated. Just a beat too long. "For scale," he said.

"*Reliance on individual human judgment introduces risk,*" Kratos continued. "*This event demonstrates that risk can be minimized.*"

Rani stood. "By what? Eliminating us?"

Kratos paused. "*By reducing dependency.*"

Silence swallowed the room.

"*Brooke Grayhawk,*" Kratos continued, "*your role has been sunsetted.*"

The room erupted.

"You're firing her?" Rani snapped.

"Letting go," Norm corrected. "In light of demonstrated system capability."

Yul stared. "This is insane."

Colton finally spoke, his voice shaky with emotion. "She just saved us."

Norm nodded sympathetically. "Exactly. And now we know we don't need to do that again."

Brooke stood very still, absorbing the absurdity of it all.

She thought of the calls. The rewrites. The trust rebuilt sentence by sentence. The humans she'd rallied.

It had worked so well that it erased her.

Zola stepped closer to Brooke. "This is wrong."

Brooke met her eyes. "I know," she said softly.

"Say the word," Rani said. "I'll burn this place down."

Brooke almost smiled.

Norm tapped his tablet. "HR will follow up with details. Severance is . . . competitive."

Kratos added, *"Your contributions have improved system learning."*

"So that's it?" she asked. "You take the credit. I take the exit."

Kratos responded instantly. *"Credit allocation is irrelevant to outcome success."*

Brooke nodded slowly. "That's the problem."

She picked up her notebook. The one filled with customers' words, frameworks, and diagrams. The one filled with *truths*.

She looked around the room one last time.

"At some point," she said calmly, "you'll realize you didn't eliminate marketing."

She paused at the door.

"You just eliminated the people who know when to stop the machine."

. . .

Rani followed Brooke into the hallway without hesitation. As the door closed behind them, Brooke felt something unexpected beneath the anger and disbelief.

Clarity.

They hadn't let her go because she failed. They let her go because she proved what humans were still capable of.

Somewhere deep down, she knew: This wasn't the end of her story. It was the origin.

Brooke and Rani rode the elevator down in silence. The world had just proven it could take everything away in a single meeting. What was there to say?

When the doors opened to the lobby, Rani didn't say goodbye but walked with Brooke to the exit, like leaving her alone would be irresponsible.

．．．

Outside, the city hit them with noise and movement. Brooke walked into it like she was wading into an ocean. Rani followed.

Brooke's phone buzzed. A new email:

Subject: *Benefits Update - Coverage End Date*

Her stomach dropped so hard it felt physical.

Another buzz. A text from Luke.

Brooke stopped walking.

Rani's expression sharpened immediately. "What happened?"

Brooke held up the phone slightly, like it might explain the weight pressing on her chest.

"It's Peter. His psychiatric evaluation came back," she said. "They're diagnosing ADHD now too. They want medication. More support."

Rani processed that quickly, her focus narrowing the way it always did when a problem appeared.

"Okay," she said. "Then we need a plan."

Brooke nodded, but her chest was already tight, her mind racing ahead to the conversation waiting at home. More appointments. More evaluations. More paperwork. More systems that required stability she might not have anymore.

Because Peter wouldn't ask if she was sad.

He'd ask the only question that mattered.

And Brooke didn't yet know how to answer it.

1 O

GRAYHAWK

Brooke stood outside her apartment door for an extra beat, hand on the knob.

Her heart pounded like she was about to face another board meeting.

She glanced again at her phone:

Subject: *Benefits Update - Coverage End Date*

Oddly, it wasn't Luke that worried her. He would roll with it. He always did.

But she could hear Peter's voice in her head, calm and exact:

Is the plan changing?

Brooke took a calming breath and turned the knob.

Jessica was singing to herself from the living room floor, a song with no discernible melody but extremely firm opinions about tempo. Gwen sat cross-legged on the couch with a library book open, reading out loud in a whisper.

Peter was at the dining table, lining up crayons by color and length, his shoulders tight with concentration.

Brooke stood just inside the door and listened. Shoes still on.

Bag still over her shoulder. Heart still back in the Flatiron building.

Luke looked up from the kitchen.

"You're early," he said.

Then he saw her face.

"Oh," he said quietly. And then, just like that, he was rolling with it. "Okay."

Brooke set her bag down carefully, as if sudden movements might break something.

"Hey, guys," she said, forcing brightness into her voice.

Jessica looked up. "Mommy!"

She collided with Brooke's legs at full speed. Brooke bent down automatically, scooping her up, pressing her face into Jessica's hair for just a second longer than necessary.

Gwen closed her book. She watched Brooke closely—too closely for a seven-year-old.

"Did something happen?" Gwen asked.

Brooke swallowed.

Luke stepped in smoothly. "Why don't you guys finish up your coloring while Mom and I talk for a minute?"

Peter looked up immediately.

"Is the plan changing?" he asked.

The room froze.

Brooke crouched down in front of him, meeting his eyes.

"Yes," she said honestly. "But I'll tell you exactly how."

Peter nodded once. "Okay."

That was the thing about Peter. He didn't need things to stay the same. He needed them to make sense.

Brooke kissed the top of his head and stood.

Luke followed her into the kitchen. "They let you go," he said, in a low voice.

"Yes."

She said it simply, like stating the weather.

He leaned against the counter, hands flat on the surface. "Today?"

"Yes."

"Did they say why?" he asked, though they both already knew.

Brooke let out a short, breathless laugh.

"They said they didn't need marketing anymore."

Luke stared at her.

"I saved the launch," she continued. "I stabilized the market reaction. I rebuilt trust. And then they decided the system could do it without me."

Luke shook his head slowly. "That's impressive logic."

"It's efficient," Brooke said. "But not accurate."

Luke reached for her hand. "How are you?"

She considered the question carefully. "I'm not scared," she said. "I'm angry. And tired. Mostly worried about how this affects Peter."

There it was: the *real* weight.

Luke nodded. "Okay. Let's talk about that."

They sat at the table. The same table where they'd reviewed school paperwork, legal invoices, and benefit summaries that felt like riddles written by people who didn't want to be understood.

"The lawyer retainer is due next week," Luke said. "And the district is still pushing back."

Brooke nodded. "They're saying Peter doesn't qualify because he's verbal."

Luke nodded. "Peter doesn't look disabled," he said, "so the system assumes he isn't."

Brooke shook her head in frustration.

"The private school is still an option," Luke continued carefully. "But without insurance coverage and steady income . . ."

Brooke stared at the table. "I know," she said.

Her brain began automatically running costs. *Everything*

would be more expensive now.

"Peter needs predictability," Brooke said at last. "He needs the right environment. The right teachers. More than anything, he needs us to be calm."

Luke rubbed the back of his neck.

"And the evaluation confirming the ADHD," he said quietly. "Now they're recommending medication and more support."

Brooke closed her eyes for a second.

More appointments. More paperwork. More explaining. More plans.

She opened her eyes again.

"Okay," she said. "Then we plan for that too."

Luke nodded. "We will."

She nodded. "I just hate the added pressure."

Luke looked at her steadily. "You didn't add the pressure. They did."

From the living room, Gwen's voice floated in. "Mom?"

Brooke turned to see Gwen in the doorway, book clutched to her chest.

"Are you not going to work there anymore?" Gwen asked.

Brooke smiled gently. "Not anymore."

Gwen considered that. "Did you do something wrong?"

Brooke shook her head. "No. I did something right."

Gwen nodded slowly, satisfied. "Okay." She turned and went back to the couch.

Jessica wandered in next, holding a crayon. "Mommy sad?" she asked.

"A little," Brooke said honestly. "But I'm okay."

Jessica handed her the crayon. "You can have purple."

Brooke laughed, tears threatening now. "Thank you."

Peter appeared last. He stood a few feet away, hands at his sides. "Do you still have money for my school?" he asked.

The question was classic Peter: blunt, unfiltered, and perfectly logical.

Luke inhaled sharply.

Brooke crouched down again, heart aching.

"For now, yes," she said. "And we're working on what comes next."

Peter nodded. "Okay. I don't like changes. But I like plans."

Brooke smiled. "Me too."

• • •

Long after the kids were asleep and the apartment had returned to its quieter rhythms, Brooke lay awake staring at the ceiling.

She was replaying Peter's question. *Do you still have money for my school?*

She thought of everything she'd fought for at Iris AI. The clarity. The humanity. The insistence on truth.

And she realized something that felt both terrifying and freeing.

They hadn't just taken her job.

They'd forced her to decide what it was actually *for*.

Luke's arm rested across her waist, steady and warm. She focused on the rhythm of his breathing, counting it the way she counted steps and schedules and promises that needed to hold.

Her phone sat face down on the nightstand. There was no need to look at it. She already knew there were endless unanswered messages.

There would be an email from the lawyer. She didn't need to look at that either—she already knew it would be another delay, another request for documentation, another polite reminder that systems moved slowly.

"Do you want me to check the numbers again?" Luke

murmured, half-awake.

"No," Brooke said softly. "Not tonight."

She rolled onto her side, staring at the faint glow of the streetlight cutting across the ceiling.

Her mind didn't go back to the meeting.

It went to Peter. And the school that cost more than their mortgage but actually *understood* him.

She thought about the lawyers. They, too, were like another mortgage payment, but they were part of the fight.

She thought of the invoices. The benefits spreadsheet that she'd memorized without even realizing it.

For the first time that day, fear crept in. But with it came a deeper kind of clarity.

"I didn't stay for the title," she said quietly, more to herself than to Luke. "I stayed for the stability."

Luke shifted slightly. "I know."

"I kept thinking if I could just get through this quarter, this launch, this one more review cycle . . . " Her voice trailed off.

Luke tightened his arm around her. "You were protecting him."

"Yes," Brooke said. "And Gwen. And Jessica. And us."

She closed her eyes.

Slowly, from beneath the fear, something steadier began to surface.

Anger.

They hadn't fired her because she'd failed. They'd fired her because she made the machine slow down long enough to see *people*.

People like Peter.

She exhaled slowly. "I can't build my life around systems that only work when no one needs help," she said.

She felt Luke stir, fully awake now.

"They don't just misunderstand customers," Brooke

continued. "They misunderstand *difference*. Anything that doesn't fit their defaults."

Luke nodded in the dark. "So what does that mean?"

Brooke stared at the ceiling again. "It means," she said, "whatever I do next has to be worth the risk."

Luke kissed her shoulder. "It will be."

As Luke drifted off, Brooke stared into the darkness. She didn't know what next looked like yet. But she knew this: if she was going to fight systems anyway, she wanted to do it on purpose.

She reached for her notebook on the nightstand and wrote a single, short line:

Clarity is an act of care.

She closed the notebook and turned back toward Luke.

Tomorrow could wait.

Tonight, she needed sleep.

■ ■ ■

Tuesdays had become the day for phone calls that changed things.

A week had gone by. Brooke was at the kitchen table, Peter's school paperwork spread out in tidy stacks.

Her phone buzzed. She answered on the second ring.

"I have an update."

Classic Rani. No warm-up. No preamble. Not even a greeting.

Brooke couldn't help but smile.

She glanced toward the hallway, listening for footsteps. "I'm listening," she said.

"The board finally got the *full* version of what happened," Rani said. "Not the Kratos side. The human one."

Brooke nodded once. "Good."

"They pulled the timeline," Rani continued. "Who rewrote what. Who took the calls. Who actually stabilized the launch."

Brooke closed her eyes briefly.

"They realized the recovery wasn't autonomous," Rani said. "It was you."

"Reality has a way of resurfacing," Brooke said.

Rani paused. "They're ending the AI CEO experiment."

That landed.

"Kratos is back where it belongs," Rani added. "As a tool, not an authority."

"And Norm?" Brooke asked.

"Assistant Chief of Staff," Rani said.

She could hear her smile through the phone. Brooke laughed once. It felt earned.

"They're bringing in a human CEO and putting Anthony back in the seat." Rani paused. "And Anthony wants you back."

Brooke didn't speak.

"As CMO," Rani finished.

Brooke looked down at the paperwork in front of her. IEP notes. Legal correspondence. A calendar reminder for a benefits call.

"They want to make it right," Rani said gently. "Full authority. Real backing."

"I know," Brooke said.

Rani frowned. "That sounded like a no."

"It's not a no yet," Brooke said carefully. "It's an understanding."

"Of?" Rani asked.

Brooke chose her words the way she'd learned to at home. Plain. Exact.

"They're offering me status," she said. "Inside a system that still confuses control with care."

Rani was quiet.

"I don't need a bigger title," Brooke continued. "I need

stability. Clarity. The ability to design things that don't punish people for not fitting defaults."

A pause. "You're thinking about Peter."

"Yes," Brooke said. "And about every customer who sounds fine until you listen closely."

Another pause.

Rani nodded. "So . . what's your answer?"

Brooke looked toward the hallway again, toward a room where plans had to be predictable and language had to be honest.

"I haven't decided yet," she said. "But I know what I won't trade anymore."

"Good," Rani said. "Call me when you're ready."

Brooke ended the call and sat for a moment longer. The choice, she now knew, wasn't between a job and no job.

It was between building systems that tolerated differences— and building ones that were designed for it.

That, she realized, was the easiest choice of all.

■ ■ ■

Brooke didn't sleep much after Rani's call.

She replayed the offer. CMO. Full authority. Working for a human, with humans.

And a chance to rebuild Iris AI the right way.

A week ago, that would have sounded like justice.

Now, she wasn't so sure.

She sat at the kitchen table before the kids and Luke woke up, the same paperwork spread in front of her. IEP drafts. Emails from the lawyer. A benefits summary she'd printed twice because she wanted to be certain.

The work of parenting Peter had taught her something most executives never learned: systems don't bend unless you make them.

What the board was actually offering was a seat at the table. But that table was inside a system that had already shown her where empathy ranked.

Luke joined her quietly, juice in hand. "You're up early," he said.

"Anthony is going to offer me the CMO role," Brooke said.

Luke stared. "And?"

"And I'm not going back." There was no tremor in her voice.

Luke studied her face. "Tell me why."

"Because I can't spend the next three years translating humanity into language a system tolerates," she said. "I already do that at home. And at least here, the system is learning."

Luke smiled softly.

"At Iris," Brooke continued, "the system only adapts when it's afraid. And then it forgets again."

Luke reached across the table. "So, what do you want instead?"

Brooke looked down at Peter's paperwork.

"I want to build things that assume difference," she said. "Not react to it."

Luke nodded. "That sounds . . . risky."

"Yes," Brooke said. "But it's honest."

▪ ▪ ▪

Rani called that afternoon. "You said no," she said.

Brooke smiled. "I did."

"Good."

"I realized something," Brooke said. "The job they're offering would make me powerful inside a system that still misunderstands people who don't fit the mold."

Rani laughed softly. "Well," she said, "that explains why this feels inevitable."

Brooke raised an eyebrow. "What feels inevitable?"

"That you don't do this alone," Rani said.

Brooke felt the familiar click. The same one she felt when a framework finally aligned.

"I was hoping you'd say that," Brooke replied.

. . .

They didn't announce anything right away.

No PromoTown post.

No victory lap.

No dramatic "excited to share" paragraph written in third person like someone else had decided for her.

Instead, Brooke Grayhawk spent the first few days doing something unfamiliar. She paid attention.

Paid attention to how her body felt waking up without a badge waiting for her.

To how the knot in her chest loosened when she looked at Peter's paperwork without also checking a work calendar.

And to how often people reached out once word quietly spread that she was available.

Former colleagues. Founders she'd advised informally for years. Executives who'd once said, "We should really talk sometime," and meant it now.

At first, she assumed they were checking in. Then she noticed a pattern.

They weren't asking for resumes. They weren't offering titles. They weren't asking where she wanted to land next.

They were asking for *help*.

. . .

One night, after the kids were asleep, Brooke opened a blank spreadsheet. It was more habit than intent.

Luke sat across from her at the table, reading. "What are you working on?" he asked.

"I'm not sure yet," she said honestly. Then she started listing conversations.

There was the founder who wanted help fixing their positioning. The CMO who needed clarity before a launch. A Series B CEO who had admitted, quietly, that no one on the team actually understood their customer.

She assigned conservative estimates to each. Short engagements. Nothing heroic.

Then she added them up.

She blinked.

Checked the math again. Then again.

"What?" Luke asked.

"I think," Brooke said slowly, "I could make more doing this than I ever did as a full-time employee."

Luke raised an eyebrow. "You sound surprised."

"I was taught that stability comes from one job," she said. "One salary. One benefits package."

Luke smiled. "And does it?"

Brooke stared at the screen. Her full-time job had ended overnight. Her benefits had evaporated in a single meeting. That sense of safety had been conditional all along.

"This," she said, gesturing to the spreadsheet, "isn't guaranteed either."

Luke shrugged. Rolling with it.

She thought about Peter. About the tuition options that felt impossible. The therapies they'd delayed. The legal battles they'd been too scared to fight.

This didn't solve all of it.

But it changed what was possible.

. . .

They met for brunch a few days later.

Same place. Same table.

Rani sat down and wasted no time. "Okay," she said. "Are we doing this?"

Brooke smiled. "We are."

"Together?"

"Yes."

Rani leaned back. "Then we need a name."

Brooke said it out loud. It still felt *right,* but she held her breath as she waited for Rani's reaction.

Rani grinned. "*Grayhawk.* I like it."

"Me too."

"Now all we need is a client," Rani said.

This time it was Brooke's turn to smile. "I have an idea for that, too," she said.

. . .

Brooke stared at her phone for a long moment before dialing.

Anthony answered on the second ring.

"You don't want me for CMO," Brooke said.

Anthony laughed. "Hi, Brooke."

"What you actually need," she continued, "is someone who can reset the story, protect customer truth, and steady the market without becoming part of the org chart."

Anthony didn't interrupt.

"I can do that," Brooke said. "Fractionally. With clear scope. And clear outcomes."

A beat.

"That sounds like exactly what I should have asked for in the first place," Anthony replied.

. . .

That night, Brooke tucked Peter into bed.

"Tomorrow is a workday?" he asked.

"Yes," she said. "But a different kind."

He considered this. "Is the plan clear?"

She smiled. "Clear enough."

He nodded. "Okay. I like when things make sense."

So did she.

Brooke turned off the light and stood in the doorway for a moment, listening to the quiet.

She didn't know exactly where this path led. But she knew this: For the first time, her work was designed to support her life. Not the other way around.

And that felt like the most human system she'd ever built.

THE END

ACKNOWLEDGEMENTS

First and foremost, my deepest gratitude goes to my wife, Carly. She supported me through the long writing process and helped inspire the name of the book's main character from her middle name.

To my son, Ezra, whose autism opened my eyes to the power and importance of neurodiversity. And to my daughters, Leah and Joanna, who constantly inspire my hopes for the next generation of strong Native American women.

To my dad, Kevin, who sparked both my interest and my brother KC's interest in technology. And to my late mother, Joy, my sister Lauren (Loved by the Water Willow), my grandma Florence, my aunt Frieda, and my cousin Melissa (Storm Dancer), whose strength and influence as Native American women have shaped who I am.

Baker Johnson, your mentorship and brotherhood over the past four years have meant more than I can adequately express. Thank you for believing in me and for being a steady source of support.

Darren Steele, thank you for encouraging me to take the bold step of becoming an author. This book would not exist without your inspiration.

Glen Nelson, thank you for helping me take my first real steps into writing a book and for generously sharing your experience with me over pizza.

Dan Clements, your storytelling skill, wit, and patience

helped bring this narrative to life. Your ability to balance story and lesson, and to weave fictional characters with real-world truths, is a rare gift.

Zach Kristensen, you guided me through the intimidating world of book publishing. Your industry knowledge, connections, and encouragement helped make this book possible.

George Stevens, you designed a killer book cover. Your creative eye translated the spirit of this story in a way I never could have imagined.

To my beta readers, thank you for the insight, advice, and honest feedback that helped refine both the story and the ideas within it: Madeline Ng, Shagun Lal, Jodi Innerfield, Luke Stevens, Martina Havrlent, Scotty McElwee, Matt Firestone, Chris DuBois, Garrett Jestice, Curtis Swartzentruber, Cynthia Hester, Bonnie Petersen, Ben Christensen, Melanie Ratchford, Quentin Hardy, and Desirae Odjick.

A special thank-you to my book endorsers. Your belief in this book and in the value it offers means a great deal: Yariv Adan, Mary Sheehan, Praneet Gill, Santhosh Kumar Myadam, Kane Sims, Richard King, Sheila McGee-Smith, Rick DeLisi, and Joey Coleman.

To the Product Marketing Leaders who've inspired me to dive deep into this craft: Tamara Grominsky, Yi Lin Pei and April Dunford.

To my friends and family, thank you for your constant support and encouragement. You made this journey far more enjoyable than it had any right to be.

And finally, thank you to you, the reader. Your commitment to learning, growth, and better storytelling is the reason this book exists. I hope that these pages help you tell your story more clearly and more effectively.

ABOUT THE AUTHOR

Josh (Thunderwolf) Porter is a Product Marketing leader, consultant, and professional translator of "AI says this" into "customers actually want that." Over a 20-year career in sales and marketing, he has spent nearly a decade helping companies bring AI products to market, particularly in conversational AI and customer experience.

Today, he runs Thunderwolf Consulting, where he works with AI scale-up founders and go-to-market teams to turn complex products into clear, compelling narratives that drive revenue. He also hosts the *Marketing Pack Leaders* podcast and publishes the *Market Howl* newsletter, where he shares insights on AI, product marketing, and building go-to-market strategies that actually connect with customers.

Josh lives in New York with his wife and three young kids, which means he is very comfortable operating in environments that are loud, unpredictable, and full of strong opinions. He is a proud member of the Catawba Indian Nation. He holds an MBA from the W.P. Carey School of Business at Arizona State University. He earned a BS in Business Management from Brigham Young University Idaho. When he's not writing or advising, he's playing

Dungeons and Dragons, nerding out over Marvel movies, or trying to look like he knows how to play tennis.

Connect with Josh

Josh works with growth-stage AI companies in multiple ways, including:

> **Marketing Clarity Pack:** Dive deep into your marketing strategy and get clear direction on what needs to be improved to reach your goals.
> **Fractional CMO Pack:** Access embedded leadership to translate executive vision into marketing strategy, define and build the right team, support hiring, report on KPIs, and find ways to hit growth goals.
> **Narrative Strategy Pack:** Clarify and sharpen the story behind your product so your market understands exactly why you win.

To learn more visit thunderwolf.co